Better Homes and Gardens®
WHAT'S FOR DINNER?

110 Meals for Busy Families

Better Homes and Gardens® Books
Des Moines, Iowa

BETTER HOMES AND GARDENS® BOOKS
An Imprint of Meredith® Books

WHAT'S FOR DINNER?
Editor: Jennifer Darling
Contributing Editors: Joy Taylor, David Walsh
Recipe Writer: Marge Steenson
Associate Art Director and Illustrator:
 Lynda Haupert
Electronic Production Coordinator:
 Paula Forest
Test Kitchen Product Supervisor:
 Marilyn Cornelius
Food Stylists: Lynn Blanchard,
 Jennifer Peterson, Janet Pittman
Photographers: Mike Dieter, Scott Little
Production Manager: Douglas Johnston

Vice-President and Editorial Director:
 Elizabeth P. Rice
Executive Editor: Kay Sanders
Art Director: Ernest Shelton
Managing Editor: Christopher Cavanaugh
Test Kitchen Director: Sharon Stilwell

President, Book Group: Joseph J. Ward
Vice-President Retail Marketing: Jamie Martin
Vice-President Direct Marketing:
 Timothy Jarrell

On the cover: Cincinnati-Style Chili, page 118

Meredith Corporation
Chairman of the Executive Committee:
 E.T. Meredith III
Chairman of the Board and Chief Executive
 Officer: Jack D. Rehm
President and Chief Operating Officer:
 William T. Kerr

WE CARE!

All of us at Better Homes and Gardens® Books are dedicated to providing you with the information and ideas you need to create tasty foods. We welcome your comments and suggestions. Write us at: Better Homes and Gardens® Books, Cookbook Editorial Department, RW240, 1716 Locust Street, Des Moines, IA 50309-3023

If you would like to order additional copies of any of our books, call 1-800-678-2803 or check with your local bookstore.

Our seal assures you that every recipe in *What's for Dinner?* has been tested in the Better Homes and Gardens® Test Kitchen. This means that each recipe is practical and reliable, and meets our high standards of taste appeal. We guarantee your satisfaction with this book for as long as you own it.

WHAT'S FOR DINNER? INTRODUCTION

Versatility. That's the key to putting delectable dinners on the table night after night, even during the work week. *What's for Dinner?* offers recipe and menu options that let you tailor meal preparation to your schedule.

■ Need a meal in 30 minutes or less? Turn to chapter 1 for delicious fast food.

■ The easy-cooking recipes in chapter 2 wait on you. Relax while they're in the oven or crockery cooker.

■ Four meal-starter mixes in chapter 3 form the core for 14 fantastic dinners. Prepare the mixes today for fast, fuss-free dinners later.

■ On a weekend day or free evening, prepare one or more of the make-ahead recipes in chapter 4. Then on a harried work day, just pull a sensational dinner from your fridge or freezer.

Every recipe in *What's for Dinner?* has been perfected by the Better Homes and Gardens® Test Kitchen so you know each one will taste terrific. *What's for Dinner?* has the answers that on-the-go families are searching for: Delicious recipes for different situations every night of the week.

CONTENTS

CHAPTER ONE
6

30-MINUTE MEALS

CHAPTER TWO
88

SO-EASY COOKING

CHAPTER THREE 144

JUMP-START RECIPES

CHAPTER FOUR 176

MAKE-AHEAD DINNERS

30-MINUTE MEALS

Have Diners to Dinner Lickety Split

Enjoy fast food every night of the week—and feel good about doing it. How? By serving the recipes in this chapter. From sizzling stir-fries to sumptuous sandwiches, you'll be cooking when you prepare any of the 40 recipes found here. Start time to serve time is never more than 30 minutes, and often much less. With each recipe you try, you'll marvel at how quickly it goes together. And the taste? Well, don't be surprised if these recipes become family favorites—requested again and again.

CHICKEN BREASTS WITH RASPBERRY SAUCE

For a super-quick yet elegant meal, make these two 5-minute side dishes. Prepare one 6.25-ounce package quick-cooking long grain and wild rice mix according to label directions. (Raspberry lovers, double the raspberry sauce ingredients for the entrée so you'll have extra to drizzle over the cooked rice.) In the microwave oven cook peeled baby carrots (about 2 cups) with 2 tablespoons water, covered, about 5 minutes or till crisp-tender. A sprinkling of fresh raspberries completes each plate.

4 skinless, boneless chicken breast halves (about 1 pound)	¼ teaspoon pepper
½ teaspoon dried thyme, crushed	Nonstick spray coating
½ teaspoon dried sage, crushed	¼ cup seedless raspberry jam*
¼ teaspoon salt	2 tablespoons orange juice
	2 tablespoons wine vinegar

1 Rinse chicken; pat dry with paper towels. Combine thyme, sage, salt, and pepper; rub over chicken pieces, coating evenly.

2 Spray a 10-inch skillet with nonstick coating. Add chicken to skillet. Cook chicken over medium heat for 8 to 10 minutes or till tender and no longer pink, turning once. Remove from skillet; keep warm.

3 Stir together jam, orange juice, and vinegar; add to skillet. Boil gently, uncovered, about 2 minutes or till sauce is reduced to desired consistency. Serve chicken with sauce. Makes 4 servings.

*Note: Don't have seedless raspberry jam? Then stir regular raspberry jam to soften and press through a strainer to remove seeds.

Per serving: 185 calories, 4 g total fat (1 g saturated), 59 mg cholesterol, 189 mg sodium, 15 g carbohydrate, 0 g fiber, 22 g protein.
Daily Values: 0% vitamin A, 6% vitamin C, 1% calcium, 8% iron.

CHICKEN AND SAUSAGE COUSCOUS

6 ounces fully cooked smoked sausage (such as Polish sausage or Kielbasa), halved lengthwise and sliced into ½-inch pieces
2 stalks celery, sliced (1 cup)
2 medium carrots, thinly sliced (1 cup)
1⅓ cups chicken broth

1 cup couscous
4 ounces boneless, skinless chicken breast, cut into bite-size strips
1 medium green sweet pepper, cut into strips (¾ cup)
1 cup chicken broth
1 tablespoon cornstarch

Pick up a package of crisp bread sticks to go alongside this meal. For dessert try something light such as lemon or orange sherbet served with slices of cold, crisp melon—perfect palate refreshers.

1 In a 10-inch skillet cook and stir sausage, celery, and carrots over medium-high heat about 5 minutes or till sausage is brown. Reduce heat; cover and cook for 3 to 5 minutes more or till carrots are nearly tender. Drain off fat.

2 Meanwhile, in a medium saucepan bring the 1⅓ cups broth to boiling. Stir in couscous; cover and remove from heat. Let stand while preparing meat and vegetable mixture.

3 Add chicken and green pepper to skillet; cook and stir over medium-high heat for 3 to 5 minutes or till chicken no longer is pink. Combine the 1 cup broth and cornstarch; stir into skillet. Cook and stir over medium heat till thickened and bubbly; cook and stir for 2 minutes more. Fluff couscous with a fork. Serve sausage mixture over couscous. Makes 4 servings.

Note: In a real time crunch? Then get a jump start on dinner by cutting up the vegetables, sausage, and chicken the night before. Refrigerate them in covered containers till needed.

Per serving: 400 calories, 15 g total fat (5 g saturated), 44 mg cholesterol, 900 mg sodium, 44 g carbohydrate, 9 g fiber, 21 g protein.
Daily Values: 85% vitamin A, 41% vitamin C, 4% calcium, 13% iron.

SWEET AND SOUR CHICKEN

6 ounces rice noodles or 2 cups hot
    cooked rice
1 8-ounce can pineapple chunks
    (juice pack)
¾ cup chicken broth
¼ cup vinegar
3 tablespoons brown sugar
2 tablespoons cornstarch
2 tablespoons soy sauce
1 tablespoon cooking oil

½ teaspoon bottled minced garlic or
    1 clove garlic, minced
1 cup sliced celery
1 medium onion, cut into thin
    wedges
1 small red or green sweet pepper,
    cut into thin bite-size strips
12 ounces skinless, boneless chicken
    breasts, cut into bite-size strips

1 Break rice noodles into a large bowl, if using; cover with warm water. Let stand for 15 minutes while preparing chicken mixture.

2 Drain pineapple, reserving juice (you should have about ⅓ cup). For sauce, in a small bowl stir together the reserved pineapple juice, the chicken broth, vinegar, brown sugar, cornstarch, and soy sauce. Set aside.

3 Heat the oil in a wok or large skillet over medium-high heat. (Add more oil as necessary during cooking.) Stir-fry garlic in hot oil for 15 seconds. Add celery and onion; stir-fry for 2 minutes. Add the sweet pepper; stir-fry for 2 minutes more. Remove vegetables from wok.

4 Add the chicken to the hot wok. Stir-fry for 2 to 3 minutes or till no longer pink. Stir sauce; add to wok. Cook and stir till thickened and bubbly. Add cooked vegetables and pineapple. Cook and stir for 2 minutes more or till heated through. Drain rice noodles, if using; arrange noodles or hot cooked rice on 4 dinner plates. Top with chicken mixture. Makes 4 servings.

Per serving: 388 calories, 6 g total fat (1 g saturated), 45 mg cholesterol, 706 mg sodium, 64 g carbohydrate, 2 g fiber, 19 g protein.
Daily Values: 22% vitamin A, 75% vitamin C, 5% calcium, 16% iron.

Less familiar to American cooks than rice or pasta, rice noodles are a terrific timesaver because they need no cooking. Just let them stand in warm water about 15 minutes to rehydrate. You can use them as you would pasta or rice with a saucy mixture on top or plain. Look for these Chinese noodles in the Oriental section of your supermarket. And while you're there, pick up some fortune cookies, too. Maybe you'll get a great fortune to go along with the guaranteed great meal.

CHICKEN CHOP SUEY

4 skinless, boneless chicken breast
    halves (about 1 pound)
1¼ cups chicken broth or beef broth
2 tablespoons cornstarch
2 tablespoons soy sauce
1 tablespoon molasses
½ teaspoon ground ginger
1 tablespoon cooking oil

2 cups sliced celery
1 medium onion, chopped
2 cups fresh bean sprouts or one
    16-ounce can bean sprouts,
    drained
Chow mein noodles or hot
    cooked rice

1 Rinse chicken; pat dry. Cut into ½-inch pieces. For sauce, stir together the broth, cornstarch, soy sauce, molasses, and ginger; set aside.

2 Heat the oil in a wok or large skillet over medium-high heat. (Add more oil as necessary during cooking.) Stir-fry the celery and onion in hot oil for 2 minutes. Add fresh bean sprouts, if using, and stir-fry for 1 to 2 minutes more or till celery and onion are crisp-tender. Remove vegetables from wok or skillet.

3 Add half of the chicken to the hot wok. Stir-fry for 3 to 4 minutes or till no longer pink. Remove chicken from the wok. Repeat with remaining chicken. Return all chicken and cooked vegetables to the wok; push from the center of the wok. Stir sauce; add to the center of the wok. Cook and stir till thickened and bubbly. Add canned bean sprouts, if using. Stir to coat with sauce. Cook and stir about 1 minute more or till heated through. Serve immediately over chow mein noodles or hot cooked rice. Makes 4 servings.

Per serving: 346 calories, 14 g total fat (3 g saturated fat), 60 mg cholesterol, 28 g carbohydrate, 3 g fiber, 27 g protein.
Daily Values: 1% vitamin A, 19% vitamin C, 4% calcium, 20% iron.

If you crave dessert, serve quarters of fresh pineapples, and drizzle them with chocolate syrup, if you like. Don't forget a pot of hot herbal tea.

The most time-consuming part about stir-frying is cutting up the meats and vegetables before cooking. Fortunately, most supermarkets carry many foods ready for stir-frying. In the produce section, look for cut-up vegetables such as broccoli, carrots, cauliflower, and mushrooms. In the meat section, check out the stir-fry strips of meat. Any of these fresh products will save you time in the kitchen.

STIR-FRY CHICKEN WITH FETA

Brighten each serving by accompanying the main dish with micro-cooked zucchini and yellow summer squash slices drizzled with olive oil and lemon juice.

12 ounces skinless, boneless chicken breasts
1 cup orzo (about 6 ounces) or 1 cup couscous
⅓ cup chicken broth
2 tablespoons wine vinegar
1 tablespoon cornstarch
Nonstick spray coating
1 cup chopped onion

1 teaspoon bottled minced garlic or 2 cloves garlic, minced
1 tablespoon olive oil
1 14½-ounce can Italian-style stewed tomatoes
1 teaspoon sugar
½ cup crumbled feta cheese (2 ounces)
Snipped fresh basil or chopped ripe olives (optional)

1 Rinse chicken; pat dry with paper towels. Cut chicken into thin bite-size strips; set aside.

2 Prepare orzo or couscous according to package directions. Combine broth, vinegar, and cornstarch; set aside.

3 Meanwhile, spray a 10-inch skillet with nonstick coating. Stir-fry onion and garlic over medium-high heat for 2 minutes. Remove from skillet. Add oil; stir-fry chicken for 3 to 4 minutes or till no longer pink. Stir in undrained tomatoes, sugar, onion mixture, and broth mixture. Cook and stir till thickened and bubbly. Cook and stir for 2 minutes more.

4 Drain orzo or fluff couscous with a fork. Serve chicken mixture over hot orzo or couscous. Top each serving with feta cheese and, if desired, basil or olives. Makes 4 servings.

Per serving: 393 calories, 10 g total fat (3 g saturated), 57 mg cholesterol, 49 g carbohydrate, 1 g fiber, 26 g protein.
Daily Values: 11% vitamin A, 28% vitamin C, 9% calcium, 19% iron.

BROILED FISH STEAKS WITH TARRAGON CHEESE SAUCE

Serve the broiled fish on a bed of pasta such as large bow tie, linguine, or fettuccine. Add a handful of julienne strips of red sweet pepper to the pasta during the last 5 minutes it cooks. Drain the pasta and sweet peppers, then toss with olive oil; top with cracked black pepper, if desired.

1¼ **pounds fresh or frozen salmon, swordfish, or tuna steaks (about ¾ inch thick)**

½ **cup plain yogurt or light dairy sour cream**

½ **cup shredded mozzarella or Monterey Jack cheese (2 ounces)**

2 **teaspoons snipped fresh tarragon or ½ teaspoon dried tarragon, crushed**

Salt

Pepper

Fresh tarragon sprigs (optional)

1 Thaw fish, if frozen. (See tip, page 22.) Rinse fish; pat dry with paper towels. Cut fish steaks into 4 equal portions, if necessary. Stir together the yogurt or sour cream, cheese, and tarragon; set aside.

2 Place fish on unheated rack of broiler pan. Sprinkle fish with salt and pepper. Broil 4 inches from the heat for 6 to 9 minutes or till fish flakes easily with a fork. Spoon yogurt mixture over steaks. Broil 30 to 60 seconds more or till heated through and cheese starts to melt. Garnish with fresh tarragon sprigs, if desired. Makes 4 servings.

Per serving: 188 calories, 8 g total fat (3 g saturated), 36 mg cholesterol, 236 sodium, 3 g carbohydrate, 0 g fiber, 25 g protein.
Daily Values: 5% vitamin A, 0% vitamin C, 12% calcium, 6% iron.

PIZZA FISH FILLETS

1½ pounds fresh or frozen haddock, cod, or orange roughy fillets, ½ to ¾ inch thick	1 medium green sweet pepper, chopped
Nonstick spray coating	1 medium onion, chopped
½ teaspoon lemon-pepper seasoning	¼ cup water
12 ounces spinach fettuccine	1 8-ounce can pizza sauce
2 cups sliced fresh mushrooms	½ cup shredded mozzarella cheese (2 ounces)

1 Thaw fish, if frozen. (See tip, page 22.) Cut the fish into 6 serving-size pieces. Spray a 2-quart rectangular baking dish with nonstick coating. Place fish in the prepared baking dish, tucking under any thin edges so fish cooks evenly. Measure the thickness of the fish. Sprinkle the fish with the lemon-pepper seasoning.

2 Bake fish, uncovered, in a 450° oven till fish just flakes easily with a fork (allow 6 to 9 minutes per ½ inch thickness). Drain off any liquid.

3 Meanwhile, cook fettuccine according to the package directions. In a medium saucepan cook mushrooms, green pepper, and onion in the ¼ cup water, covered, about 5 minutes or just till tender. Drain; add pizza sauce. Heat through.

4 Serve fish on fettuccine; spoon sauce over fish. Sprinkle with cheese. Makes 6 servings.

Per serving: 342 calories, 4 g total fat (1 g saturated), 50 mg cholesterol, 604 mg sodium, 46 g carbohydrate, 2 g fiber, 29 g protein.
Daily Values: 19% vitamin A, 49% vitamin C, 11% calcium, 15% iron.

Frozen fruit makes a refreshingly icy dessert when served partially thawed. While the sauce for the fish is heating, set out two 10-ounce packages of frozen light-syrup-pack mixed fruit (in the quick-thaw pouch). At dessert time, spoon the fruit into wine glasses or sherbet dishes, add a splash of lemon juice, and 2 table-spoons ginger ale.

SWEET MUSTARD HALIBUT

While the fish bakes, put four brown-and-serve rolls in the oven and bake about 5 minutes or till light brown. Put your microwave oven to work for any easy meal too—cook frozen green beans or broccoli while the fish and bread bake.

1 to 1¼ pounds fresh or frozen halibut
    steaks, cut ¾ inch thick
½ cup chunky salsa

2 tablespoons honey
2 tablespoons Dijon-style mustard

1 Thaw fish, if frozen. (See tip, below.) Rinse fish; pat dry with paper towels. Measure the thickness of the fish. Arrange fish in a shallow 2-quart baking dish. Bake uncovered, in a 450° oven till fish just flakes easily with a fork (allow 6 to 9 minutes per ½ inch thickness). Drain excess liquid from fish.

2 Meanwhile, in a small bowl stir together the salsa and honey. Spread mustard over drained fish, the spoon salsa mixture atop mustard; bake for 2 to 3 minutes more or till mustard and salsa mixture are hot. Makes 4 servings.

Per serving: 176 calories, 4 g total fat (0 g saturated), 36 mg cholesterol, 362 mg sodium, 11 g carbohydrate, 0 g fiber, 24 g protein.
Daily Values: 8% vitamin A, 15% vitamin C, 4% calcium, 8% iron.

THAW FISH QUICKLY IN THE MICROWAVE OVEN

Fish is one of the fastest cooking entrées so always keep a package on hand in your freezer for those last-minute meals. To thaw 1 pound of fish in your microwave oven, place the frozen fillets or steaks in a dish and cover with vented plastic wrap. Micro-cook on 30% power (medium-low) for 6 to 9 minutes, turning and separating the fish after 3 minutes. Let fillets stand 10 minutes and steaks 15 minutes before proceeding with your recipe. For 1½ pounds fish, allow a little more microwave time. If you know you'll be fixing fish the next day, put time to work for you and thaw the fish overnight in the refrigerator.

TANGY THYME FISH

Look in your supermarket's frozen vegetable section for a 16-ounce package of vegetables featuring a colorful combination, such as broccoli, peppers, and mushrooms. While you prepare the fish, cook the vegetables in your microwave oven following package directions.

1 **pound fresh or frozen salmon, sole, flounder, cod, or orange roughy fillets, ½ to ¾ inch thick**
1 **cup chicken broth**
¼ **cup chopped onion**
⅛ **teaspoon pepper**
⅛ **teaspoon dried thyme or marjoram, crushed**

2 **tablespoons water**
1 **teaspoon cornstarch**
¼ **cup original-style buttermilk ranch salad dressing**
2 **tablespoons snipped fresh parsley**
Fresh lemon slices (optional)

1 Thaw fish, if frozen. (See tip, page 22.) Rinse fish and pat dry with paper towels. Measure the thickness of the fish.

2 In a 10-inch skillet combine the broth, onion, pepper, and thyme or marjoram. Bring to boiling. Place fish in skillet, tucking under any thin edges so fish cooks evenly. Cover and simmer for 4 to 6 minutes per ½ inch thickness or till fish flakes easily with a fork. Remove fish to a hot platter; keep warm.

3 Bring liquid in skillet to boiling; boil, uncovered, over medium-high heat for 3 to 5 minutes or till reduced to about ½ cup. Combine water and cornstarch; stir into liquid in skillet. Cook and stir till thickened and bubbly. Cook and stir 2 minutes more. Stir in salad dressing and parsley. Serve herb sauce and, if desired, lemon slices with fish. Makes 4 servings.

Per serving: 236 calories, 13 g total fat (2 g saturated fat), 50 mg cholesterol, 417 mg sodium, 3 g carbohydrate, 0 g fiber, 24 g protein.
Daily Values: 4% vitamin A, 5% vitamin C, 1% calcium, 8% iron.

SOUTHERN SEAFOOD AND RICE

2⅓ cups chicken broth
½ cup sliced green onion
1 teaspoon Worcestershire sauce
½ teaspoon dried thyme, crushed
½ teaspoon bottled minced garlic or
    1 clove garlic, minced
⅛ to ¼ teaspoon ground red pepper or
    bottled hot pepper sauce

1 14½-ounce can stewed tomatoes
    or Cajun-style stewed tomatoes
1 cup long grain rice
1 10-ounce package frozen cut okra,
    partially thawed
12 ounces fresh or frozen peeled and
    deveined shrimp or scallops
    Snipped fresh parsley

1 In a 3-quart saucepan combine the broth, green onion, Worcestershire sauce, thyme, garlic, and ground red pepper or hot pepper sauce. Bring to boiling. Stir in stewed tomatoes, rice, and okra. Return to boiling; reduce heat. Cover and simmer for 15 to 20 minutes or till rice is just tender, stirring once or twice.

2 Stir in shrimp or scallops. Cover and simmer for 3 to 5 minutes more or till shrimp turn pink and rice is tender. Stir to fluff rice. Sprinkle with parsley. Makes 4 servings.

Per serving: 329 calories, 2 g total fat (1 g saturated), 131 mg cholesterol, 1,062 mg sodium, 52 g carbohydrate, 2 g fiber, 23 g protein.
Daily Values: 20% vitamin A, 47% vitamin C, 10% calcium, 35% iron.

For a Louisiana-seasoned meal, serve this jambalaya-style main dish with corn bread sticks. Try this quick recipe: Stir together one 8½-ounce package corn muffin mix, 1 beaten egg, and one 8-ounce carton sour cream, stirring just till moistened. Grease corn bread stick pans or muffin cups; fill ⅔ full. Bake in a 400° oven for 15 to 20 minutes or till light brown. Makes 10.

RAVIOLI WITH RED CLAM SAUCE

1 **9-ounce package refrigerated cheese ravioli or cheese tortellini**
1 **14½-ounce can stewed tomatoes**
1 **6½-ounce can minced clams**
1 **medium zucchini, halved lengthwise and thinly sliced (1½ cups)**

2 **teaspoons Italian seasoning, crushed**
1 **8-ounce can tomato sauce**
1 **tablespoon cornstarch**
  Grated Parmesan cheese

1 Cook ravioli or tortellini according to package directions.

2 Meanwhile, in a medium saucepan combine stewed tomatoes, undrained clams, zucchini, and Italian seasoning. Bring to boiling; reduce heat. Simmer, uncovered, for 1 minute. Stir together the tomato sauce and cornstarch till well blended; stir into hot mixture. Cook and stir over medium heat till thickened and bubbly. Cook and stir for 2 minutes more. Serve clam sauce over hot pasta. Sprinkle Parmesan cheese over each serving. Makes 3 servings.

Per serving: 406 calories, 16 g total fat (1 g saturated), 113 mg cholesterol, 1,380 mg sodium, 46 g carbohydrate, 3 g fiber, 24 g protein.
Daily Values: 17% vitamin A, 42% vitamin C, 16% calcium, 32% iron.

Go Italian tonight. Buy a bag of ready-to-eat mixed salad greens (these are already rinsed and torn), or go by the salad bar at the grocery store and build a salad bowl for three. Personalize your salads by topping with fish-shaped pretzels or broken bagel chips. For an almost-home-made salad dressing, stir a little Dijon-style mustard into bottled Italian salad dressing. To complete your Italiano feast, serve a bottle of chianti.

CRISPY OVEN-FRIED FISH

For a country-style dinner, fix a saucepan of instant mashed potatoes to serve with the crunchy fish fillets. Perk up the mashed potatoes by stirring in one of the following:

- onion or garlic powder
- snipped chives or parsley
- diced green chili peppers
- crumbled bacon
- snipped dried tomatoes

A package of frozen broccoli spears completes your meal.

1 **pound fresh or frozen haddock, orange roughy, or cod fillets, ½ to ¾ inch thick**
Nonstick spray coating
2 **tablespoons plain yogurt or dairy sour cream**
2 **tablespoons Dijon-style mustard**

1 **tablespoon snipped fresh chives**
Dash ground red pepper
Dash chili powder
⅔ **cup fine dry bread crumbs**
2 **tablespoons margarine or butter, melted**
Fresh lemon slices (optional)

1 Thaw fish, if frozen. (See tip, page 22.) Cut fish into 4 equal portions; rinse and pat dry. Spray a baking sheet with nonstick coating.

2 In a small bowl combine yogurt or sour cream, mustard, chives, red pepper, and chili powder. Coat fish on all sides with yogurt mixture; then roll in bread crumbs to coat evenly. Place fish on baking sheet, tucking under any thin edges so fish cooks evenly. Drizzle fish with melted margarine or butter. Bake in a 450° oven for 6 to 10 minutes or till fish flakes easily with a fork. Serve immediately, with lemon slices, if desired. Makes 4 servings.

Per serving: 275 calories, 12 g total fat (3 g saturated), 44 mg cholesterol, 540 sodium, 19 g carbohydrate, 1 g fiber, 21 g protein.
Daily Values: 11% vitamin A, 4% vitamin C, 6% calcium, 11% iron.

CREOLE COD AND RICE

When your family asks, "What can I do to help?" suggest they fix a salad to cool the spicy entrée. If your greens weren't rinsed ahead, a salad spinner is a lifesaver for busy, health-conscious families. Rinse, spin, and dry in 5 minutes for crisp greens.

1 pound fresh or frozen cod fillets, about ½ inch thick
1 4.3- to 4.7-ounce envelope quick-cooking rice and pasta mix with vegetables
1 8-ounce can tomatoes, cut up
¼ teaspoon pepper
⅛ teaspoon ground red pepper (optional)
½ medium green sweet pepper, cut in strips or rings

1 Thaw fish, if frozen. (See tip, page 22.) In 10-inch skillet prepare rice mix as directed on the envelope except substitute undrained tomatoes for ½ cup of the liquid and add pepper and, if desired, red pepper to mixture. Cover and cook rice for half of the time directed on rice mix package.

2 Place fish fillets and green pepper on top of the rice mixture. Cover and cook over low heat about 10 minutes more or till fish flakes easily with a fork. Makes 4 servings.

Note: Look in the rice section or sauce section of your supermarket for the mix used in this recipe. You'll find a variety of quick-cooking rice and pasta mixes with different vegetables (and some with cheese) added. Any in the range of 4.3 to 4.7 ounces will work for this dish. Just pick what appeals to you.

Per serving: 263 calories, 5 g total fat (1 g saturated), 49 mg cholesterol, 649 mg sodium, 28 g carbohydrate, 1 g fiber, 25 g protein.
Daily Values: 22% vitamin A, 36% vitamin C, 7% calcium, 12% iron.

CATFISH OLÉ

1 to 1¼ pounds fresh or frozen
   catfish fillets, ½ to ¾ inch thick
½ cup finely crushed tortilla chips*
½ teaspoon dried oregano, crushed
¼ teaspoon garlic powder
2 tablespoons milk

1 cup shredded cheddar or Monterey
   Jack cheese (4 ounces)
   Shredded lettuce (optional)
⅔ cup chunky salsa
   Orange wedges (optional)

1 Thaw catfish, if frozen. (See tip, page 22.) Combine the crushed tortilla chips, oregano, and garlic powder. Dip fish portions in milk, then coat on all sides with tortilla mixture. Place coated fish in a shallow baking dish, tucking under any thin edges so fish cooks evenly. Sprinkle with any remaining tortilla mixture. Bake in a 450° oven for 6 minutes.

2 Top each fish portion with cheese. Return to oven and bake about 5 minutes more or till cheese melts and fish flakes easily with a fork.

3 Serve fish on shredded lettuce, if desired. Top with salsa, and, if desired, serve with orange wedges. Makes 4 servings.

*Note: To crush the tortillas, place a handful in a plastic bag and close. Pound with the flat side of a meat mallet till finely crushed. Or, use up the leftover crumbs in the bottom of an almost-empty bag of chips!

Per serving: 232 calories, 10 g total fat (6 g saturated), 74 mg cholesterol, 594 mg sodium, 7 g carbohydrate, 0 g fiber, 26 g protein.
Daily Values: 14% vitamin A, 14% vitamin C, 20% calcium, 6% iron.

Try this tasty tortilla fix-up to go with the crispy fish: Warm flour tortillas in the microwave oven or wrap them in foil and heat them along with the fish till softened. Stir a spoonful of honey and a little shredded orange peel into softened margarine or butter and serve with the tortillas.

FLANK STEAK WITH SPANISH RICE

1 14½-ounce can Mexican-style
    stewed tomatoes
1¾ cups water
    Several dashes bottled hot
      pepper sauce
1¼ cups long grain rice
1 teaspoon chili powder

½ teaspoon salt
¼ teaspoon ground cumin
¼ teaspoon pepper
   Dash ground cinnamon
1 to 1¼ pounds beef flank steak
   Snipped fresh cilantro or parsley
   (optional)

Summertime, or anytime, grill the flank steak instead of broiling. Cook the meat directly over medium coals for 18 to 22 minutes total for medium doneness, turning once. Flank steak is a lean cut of beef, so avoid overcooking it or it may become dry and tough.

1 In a 2-quart saucepan combine the stewed tomatoes, water, and hot pepper sauce. Bring to boiling. Stir in rice; return to boiling then reduce heat. Cover and simmer for 20 minutes. Remove from heat; let stand for 5 minutes.

2 Meanwhile, combine chili powder, salt, cumin, pepper, and cinnamon. Rub spice mixture into flank steak on all sides. Place steak on unheated rack of broiler pan. Broil steak 3 inches from the heat for 6 minutes. Turn and broil till desired doneness (allowing about 7 to 8 minutes more for medium-rare).

3 To serve, thinly slice flank steak diagonally across the grain. Fluff rice with a fork. Serve steak slices over rice; sprinkle with cilantro or parsley, if desired. Makes 4 to 6 servings.

Per serving: 409 calories, 9 g total fat (4 g saturated), 53 mg cholesterol, 698 mg sodium, 54 g carbohydrate, 1 g fiber, 27 g protein.
Daily Values: 9% vitamin A, 27% vitamin C, 3% calcium, 33% iron.

ZIPPY BEEF, MAC, AND CHEESE

For a fresh, pretty salad side dish, peel and section oranges and cut jicama into strips; arrange on a lettuce leaf and drizzle with an oil-and-vinegar dressing.

6 ounces elbow macaroni or
    corkscrew pasta (about 1½ cups)
12 ounces lean ground beef, pork, or
    turkey
1 tablespoon chili powder
1 15-ounce can tomato sauce

1 14½-ounce can stewed tomatoes or
    Mexican-style stewed tomatoes
4 ounces American or sharp
    American cheese, cut into small
    cubes
    Grated Parmesan cheese

1 In a 3-quart saucepan cook pasta according to package directions, except do not add salt.

2 Meanwhile, in a 10-inch skillet cook ground meat till no pink remains. Drain off fat.

3 Drain macaroni; return it to the saucepan. Stir in cooked meat, chili powder, tomato sauce, undrained stewed tomatoes, and cheese. Heat and stir over medium heat about 6 to 8 minutes or till heated through. Sprinkle Parmesan cheese on top of each serving. Makes 4 servings.

Note: If you're watching your sodium intake, use no-salt-added tomato sauce or low-salt stewed tomatoes.

Per serving: 342 calories, 15 g total fat (7 g saturated), 55 mg cholesterol, 957 mg sodium, 32 g carbohydrate, 2 g fiber, 20 g protein.
Daily Values: 22% vitamin A, 23% vitamin C, 15% calcium, 21% iron.

PASTA WITH LAMB AND FETA CHEESE

12 ounces boneless lean leg of lamb or
   beef sirloin steak
1 tablespoon olive oil or cooking oil
1 large onion, cut into wedges
1 teaspoon bottled minced garlic or 2
   cloves garlic, minced
1 6-ounce can tomato paste
½ cup tomato juice
½ cup water
¼ cup cider vinegar or red wine
   vinegar

1 teaspoon dried oregano, crushed
½ teaspoon ground cumin
¼ teaspoon ground cinnamon
1 medium zucchini, halved lengthwise and sliced (1¼ cups)
Hot cooked orzo or other pasta
Crumbled feta cheese
Chopped walnuts or snipped fresh
   parsley (optional)

On your way home from work, stop by the bakery or grocery store to pick up slices of fresh or frozen baklava, a rich phyllo pastry chock full of honey and walnuts. It's a traditional ending to a Greek meal—one taste and you'll know why it's a favorite.

1 Trim any separable fat from meat. Thinly slice meat across the grain into bite-size pieces. Heat oil in a 10-inch skillet; stir-fry meat for 2 to 3 minutes or till no pink remains. Remove meat from skillet.

2 Add onion and garlic to skillet; stir-fry for 1 minute. Stir in tomato paste, tomato juice, water, vinegar, oregano, cumin, and cinnamon. Add zucchini; bring to boiling. Reduce heat; cover and simmer for 5 minutes or till zucchini is tender. Return meat to skillet; heat through. Serve over hot cooked orzo or other pasta; sprinkle with feta cheese and, if desired, walnuts or parsley. Makes 4 servings.

Per serving: 349 calories, 15 g total fat (5 g saturated), 51 mg cholesterol, 323 mg sodium, 36 g carbohydrate, 4 g fiber, 19 g protein.
Daily Values: 15% vitamin A, 44% vitamin C, 6% calcium, 29% iron.

CUMBERLAND PORK MEDALLIONS

Before making the entrée, start a saucepan of quick-cooking brown rice (enough for 4 servings); during the last 5 minutes of cooking add ½ cup frozen peas. Season to taste for an easy, satisfying side dish.

1 tablespoon cooking oil or olive oil
1 pound pork tenderloin, sliced crosswise into ¾-inch slices
¼ cup sliced green onion
½ cup dry red or white wine or apple juice

½ cup chicken broth
2 tablespoons currant jelly
1 teaspoon Dijon-style mustard
1 tablespoon chicken broth or water
1 teaspoon cornstarch

1 In a 10-inch skillet heat oil; cook pork slices over medium heat for 6 to 8 minutes or till centers are just slightly pink and juices run clear, turning once. Remove meat from skillet; keep warm.

2 Add green onion to skillet; cook just till tender. Add wine or apple juice and the ½ cup broth. Boil gently over medium-high heat about 4 minutes or till reduced to about ½ cup. Add jelly and mustard, stirring till jelly is melted. Combine the 1 tablespoon broth or water and cornstarch; stir into skillet. Cook and stir over medium heat till thickened and bubbly. Cook and stir for 1 minute more. Serve sauce with the pork medallions. Makes 4 servings.

Per serving: 231 calories, 8 g total fat (2 g saturated), 81 mg cholesterol, 220 mg sodium, 8 g carbohydrate, 0 g fiber, 26 g protein.
Daily Values: 1% vitamin A, 3% vitamin C, 1% calcium, 11% iron.

PORK DIANE

1 tablespoon water
1 tablespoon white wine
    Worcestershire sauce
1 teaspoon lemon juice
1 teaspoon Dijon-style mustard
1 pound boneless pork loin roast, cut
    into four ¾- to 1-inch-thick slices

1 teaspoon lemon-pepper seasoning
2 tablespoons margarine or butter
1 tablespoon snipped fresh chives or
    parsley

1 For sauce, stir together the water, Worcestershire sauce, lemon juice, and mustard; set aside.

2 Trim excess fat from pork slices. Sprinkle both sides of each piece of meat with lemon-pepper seasoning. In a 10-inch skillet heat margarine or butter; cook pork over medium heat for 6 to 10 minutes or till centers of pork pieces are just slightly pink in center and juices run clear, turning once. Remove meat to platter; cover to keep warm. Remove skillet from heat.

3 Add sauce to skillet. Stir till well blended. Pour sauce over meat; sprinkle with chives or parsley. Makes 4 servings.

Per serving: 192 calories, 13 g total fat (4 g saturated), 51 mg cholesterol, 441 mg sodium, 1 g carbohydrate, 0 g fiber, 16 g protein.
Daily Values: 7% vitamin A, 3% vitamin C, 1% calcium, 5% iron.

Meat and potato lovers will really go for this dinner—and the potatoes are easy to prepare, too. Just quarter 8 to 10 new potatoes and cook, covered, in the microwave oven with 2 tablespoons water on 100% power about 8 minutes or till tender. Drain off water. Dot potatoes with butter and snipped chives to serve. Dress up each dinner plate with a simple but stunning garnish of snipped chive stems and blossoms from your herb garden. Finally, follow this meal with a light dessert; serve lower-fat ice cream topped with fresh or frozen sliced strawberries.

PORK CHOPS WITH CHILI-APRICOT GLAZE

As long as you're cooking your entrée under the broiler, cook your vegetables under it, too. For broiled Parmesan potatoes: Cut 2 medium potatoes into ¼-inch-thick slices. Arrange potatoes on broiler pan next to meat; brush potatoes with melted margarine or butter seasoned with paprika, garlic powder, and pepper. Broil potatoes for 8 to 9 minutes; turn and sprinkle with Parmesan cheese. Broil 4 to 6 minutes more. If desired, broil strips of red or green sweet peppers, too.

¼ cup apricot jam or preserves
¼ cup chili sauce
1 tablespoon sweet-hot mustard or brown mustard
1 tablespoon water
4 boneless pork top loin chops, 1 inch thick (about 1½ pounds total)

1 For glaze, cut up any large pieces in apricot jam or preserves. In a small saucepan combine jam or preserves, chili sauce, mustard, and water. Cook and stir over medium-low heat till heated through and well blended. Remove from heat.

2 Trim excess fat from pork chops. Place chops on unheated rack of broiler pan. Broil 4 to 5 inches from heat for 8 minutes.

3 Turn pork chops; brush generously with glaze. Broil 8 to 12 minutes more or till centers are just slightly pink and juices run clear. Spoon any remaining glaze over meat before serving. Makes 4 servings.

Note: If you can't find boneless chops, purchase a 1-pound boneless pork loin roast and slice into 4 steak-like portions yourself.

Per serving: 244 calories, 9 g total fat (3 g saturated), 64 mg cholesterol, 303 mg sodium, 18 g carbohydrate, 0 g fiber, 21 g protein.
Daily Values: 2% vitamin A, 3% vitamin C, 1% calcium, 7% iron.

LIGHT LINGUINE ALLA CARBONARA

For speedy salads, buy a bag of ready-to-eat mixed greens from the produce section of your grocery store and a box of croutons. Pass cruets of red wine vinegar and olive oil to sprinkle over each serving. While the pasta water heats up, preheat your oven to bake brown-and-serve breadsticks. These bake in about 10 minutes, following package directions.

8 ounces linguine or spaghetti
    Nonstick spray coating
2 slices turkey bacon, sliced cross-
    wise into strips
1 beaten egg
1 cup evaporated skim milk

½ cup frozen peas
¼ cup chopped red sweet pepper
¼ teaspoon crushed red pepper
½ cup grated Parmesan cheese
    Black pepper

1 Cook linguine or spaghetti according to package directions.

2 Meanwhile, spray a medium saucepan with nonstick coating. Cook turkey bacon in saucepan till crisp and light brown. Drain on paper towels. Wipe saucepan clean with a paper towel.

3 For sauce, in same saucepan combine egg, evaporated milk, peas, sweet pepper, and crushed red pepper. Cook and stir over medium heat just till the mixture coats a metal spoon (about 6 minutes). Do not boil. Stir in bacon and half of the Parmesan cheese. Heat through.

4 Immediately pour sauce over hot cooked pasta; toss to coat. Transfer to a warm serving platter. Sprinkle with black pepper and remaining Parmesan cheese. Makes 4 servings.

Per serving: 383 calories, 7 g total fat (1 g saturated), 71 mg cholesterol, 56 carbohydrate, 1 g fiber, 362 mg sodium, 22 g protein.
Daily Values: 17% vitamin A, 5% vitamin C, 41% calcium, 20% iron.

CHICKEN AND RICE SOUP

Ready-to-cook mixes such as the rice mix used in this soup recipe offer busy cooks a lot of convenience. Keep several—including rice mix, noodles mixes, and potato mixes—on hand for last-minute meals. Any of these will go well with a simple entrée such as broiled fish, poultry, or meat. If you're concerned about sodium, prepare the packaged mix using about half of the seasoning packet.

For a quickie soup lunch or supper, cut up fresh vegetable sticks or purchase the cleaned and ready-to-eat vegetables at your store. Slice your favorite bread, and the meal is served!

1 6¼- or 6¾-ounce package quick-cooking long grain and wild rice mix
5 cups water
8 ounces lean ground chicken or turkey

1 12-ounce can evaporated milk, chilled*
2 tablespoons all-purpose flour
Sliced green onion (optional)

1 In a 3-quart saucepan combine the rice mix with seasoning packet and water. Bring to boiling.

2 Drop the ground chicken or turkey by small spoonfuls into the boiling mixture (about 36 pieces total). Reduce heat; cover and simmer for 5 minutes.

3 Combine chilled milk and flour till well blended; add to boiling mixture. Cook and stir till slightly thickened and bubbly. Cook and stir for 1 minute more. Sprinkle green onion over each serving, if desired. Makes 6 servings.

***Note:** Chilling the canned milk makes it easier to blend with the flour.

Per serving: 226 calories, 6 g total fat (3 g saturated), 35 mg cholesterol, 728 mg sodium, 30 g carbohydrate, 0 g fiber, 13 g protein.
Daily Values: 4% vitamin A, 3% vitamin C, 12% calcium, 9% iron.

CHICKEN NOODLE SOUP FLORENTINE

1 49½-ounce can chicken broth	2½ cups medium noodles (5 ounces)
8 ounces fresh mushrooms, sliced (3 cups)	1 9-ounce package frozen diced cooked chicken (about 2 cups)
1 cup sliced green onion	3 cups chopped fresh spinach or
1½ teaspoons fines herbes, crushed	half of a 10-ounce package
¼ teaspoon pepper	frozen chopped spinach

1 In a 4½-quart Dutch oven combine chicken broth, mushrooms, green onion, fines herbs, and pepper. Bring to boiling; add noodles. Cook and stir till the mixture returns to a boil; reduce heat.

2 Cover and boil gently for 7 to 9 minutes or till noodles are tender (do not overcook). Add chicken and spinach to soup; heat through. Serves 6.

Note: You can freeze half of the soup in a covered container for another meal. To reheat frozen soup, place in a medium saucepan over medium heat. Cover and heat through for 20 to 25 minutes, stirring occasionally.

Per serving: 222 calories, 6 g total fat (1 g saturated), 59 mg cholesterol, 866 mg sodium, 20 g carbohydrate, 1 g fiber, 22 g protein.
Daily Values: 23% vitamin A, 20% vitamin C, 5% calcium, 25% iron.

While the soup simmers, bake an easy bread and dessert in the oven. Prepare and bake a brownie mix according to package directions. Immediately sprinkle the hot brownies with almond brickle pieces and semi-sweet chocolate pieces and cool completely.

QUICK CORN CHOWDER

¾ cup sliced celery
½ cup chopped green onion
2 cups chicken broth
⅛ teaspoon pepper
1 16-ounce can whole-kernel corn, drained
1 8¾-ounce can cream-style corn

1 5-ounce can evaporated milk
5 ounces fully cooked ham, chopped (1 cup)
1 tablespoon diced pimiento (optional)
½ cup packaged instant mashed potato flakes

1 In a 2-quart saucepan combine the celery, green onion, broth, and pepper. Bring to boiling; reduce heat. Cover and simmer for 5 minutes.

2 Stir in whole-kernel corn, undrained cream-style corn, milk, ham, and, if desired, pimiento. Bring just to boiling; reduce heat. Stir in potato flakes; cook and stir till slightly thickened. Makes 4 servings.

Per serving: 453 calories, 9 g total fat (3 g saturated), 21 mg cholesterol, 1,069 mg sodium, 76 g carbohydrate, 10 g fiber, 21 g protein.
Daily Values: 9% vitamin A, 37% vitamin C, 10% calcium, 21% iron.

Pair a steaming bowl of soup with a refreshing mixed fruit salad and a warm loaf of peppered bread. For bread, snip 8 to 10 refrigerated buttermilk or multigrain biscuits in half, and randomly arrange in a greased 7½ x3½ x2-inch loaf pan; brush with milk and sprinkle generously with pepper. Bake in a 350° oven about 20 minutes or till brown. Serve warm. If you're in a real hurry, serve thick slices of whole wheat bread from the bakery.

CHICKEN AND BEEF BROTH

For recipes in this book that call for chicken or beef broth, try one of the easy-to-use convenience products—some also come in a lower-sodium variety. Instant bouillon granules or cubes come in chicken, beef, or vegetable flavors. Just mix these with water according to the package directions before using them as broth. You can buy ready-to-use canned chicken or beef broth. The cans usually contain 14½ ounces, which is about 1¾ cups of broth. If you choose to use canned condensed chicken or beef broth, before using it, dilute it with water according to the can directions.

CURRIED PUMPKIN SOUP

¾ **cup chopped green onion**
1½ **to 2 teaspoons curry powder**
¼ **cup margarine or butter**
¼ **cup all-purpose flour**
1 **16-ounce can pumpkin**

2 **cups chicken broth***
2 **cups buttermilk**
1 **cup cubed fully cooked ham***
Sliced green onion (optional)

1 In a 3-quart saucepan cook the chopped green onion and curry powder in hot margarine or butter about 2 minutes or till onion is tender. Stir in flour. Add pumpkin and broth. Cook and stir over medium heat till thickened and bubbly. Cook and stir for 1 minute more.

2 Stir in the buttermilk and ham; heat through. Top each serving with sliced green onion, if desired. Makes 4 servings.

***Note:** Buy a center cut ham slice and cube it at home. To reduce the amount of sodium in each serving, use low-sodium chicken broth and ham.

Per serving: 282 calories, 15 g total fat (4 g saturated), 24 mg cholesterol, 1,121 mg sodium, 19 g carbohydrate, 4 g fiber, 17 g protein.
Daily Values: 269% vitamin A, 15% vitamin C, 15% calcium, 18% iron.

Celebrate the arrival of fall with a bowlful of pumpkin soup served with slices of nut bread—purchased or made from a mix. For dessert, try cooked apples; if you like, fill centers of cored apples with raisins, brown sugar, and a spinkle of nutmeg. To prepare, micro-cook 4 cored apples with 2 tablespoons water in a 2-quart casserole on high for 4 to 8 minutes or till apples are tender, rearranging and basting the apples with their juices after 3 minutes. Happy autumn!

GRILLED HAM-ON-RYE SPECIAL

Serve in-season fruits with the hot sandwich—grapes or watermelon in the summer, apples or pears in the fall. Year-round, this hot sandwich will be a hit with your family. (Don't forget the chips and pickles, too.)

¼ cup Thousand Island salad dressing
1 teaspoon prepared mustard
1 cup preshredded coleslaw mix
1 tablespoon margarine or butter

8 slices rye bread
4 ounces thinly sliced fully cooked ham
4 ounces thinly sliced Swiss cheese

1 In a small bowl stir together salad dressing and mustard. Stir in coleslaw mix; mix well.

2 Spread a thin layer of margarine or butter on one side of each piece of bread; turn bread over. Top four of the bread slices with half of the ham. Spoon coleslaw mixture on evenly, and top with sliced cheese and remaining ham. Finish by topping with remaining bread slices, margarine side up.

3 Heat a large skillet or griddle. Cook sandwiches over medium-low heat for 2 to 3 minutes or till golden; turn sandwiches over. Grill 2 to 3 minutes more or till golden and cheese starts to melt. Makes 4 servings.

Per serving: 409 calories, 20 g total fat (8 g saturated), 47 mg cholesterol, 976 mg sodium, 40 g carbohydrate, 5 g fiber, 19 g protein.
Daily Values: 12% vitamin A, 31% vitamin C, 31% calcium, 14% iron.

HOT APPLE AND CHEESE SANDWICH

1 medium apple	4 slices Canadian-style bacon
4 English muffins, split	4 slices process Swiss cheese
2 tablespoons creamy Dijon-style mustard blend	1 tablespoon margarine or butter

1 Core apple and slice crosswise forming rings. Spread one side of muffin halves with mustard blend.

2 To assemble, top 4 muffin halves with a slice of bacon, 1 or 2 apple rings, a slice of cheese, and remaining muffin halves. Spread margarine lightly on outside of each sandwich.

3 Heat a large skillet or griddle. Cook sandwiches over medium-low heat about 5 minutes or till toasted. Turn; cook 4 to 5 minutes more or till toasted and cheese starts to melt. Makes 4 servings.

Per serving: 343 calories, 15 g total fat (6 g saturated), 39 mg cholesterol, 837 mg sodium, 33 g carbohydrate, 1 g fiber, 18 g protein.
Daily Values: 10% vitamin A, 10% vitamin C, 31% calcium, 11% iron.

For a quick coleslaw with a new twist, use broccoli coleslaw mix (a blend of broccoli, red cabbage, and carrot). Just add some bottled ranch salad dressing, stir, and quick-chill in the freezer while the sandwiches cook.

B.L.T. AND MORE

Just about any deli salad goes well with a B.L.T. Pick up a pint of potato salad, coleslaw, or pasta salad at the grocery store. At home, lighten the deli salad with one of these healthwise tricks:

■ Drain off excess dressing.
■ Stir in chopped broccoli, shredded cabbage, or shredded carrot to stretch the dressing.
■ Toss a saucy salad mixture with chilled cooked pasta.

¼ cup mayonnaise or salad dressing
8 slices whole grain bread, toasted
12 slices bacon or turkey bacon, cooked and drained

2 medium tomatoes, sliced
4 to 8 leaf lettuce leaves or 8 to 12 fresh spinach leaves

1 Spread mayonnaise or salad dressing on one side of each slice of toasted bread. To assemble sandwiches, top 4 bread slices with bacon, tomato, lettuce, and remaining bread slices. Cut in half to serve. Makes 4 servings.

B.L.T. with Guacamole: Prepare as above, except substitute frozen (thawed) guacamole for the mayonnaise or salad dressing.

B.L.T. with Turkey: Prepare as above, adding one or two thin slices cooked turkey breast to each sandwich (2 to 4 ounces total).

B.L.T. with Cheese: Prepare as above, adding a slice of cheese (such as harvarti with dill, white cheddar, or Jarlsburg) to each sandwich.

B.L.T. with Pesto: Prepare as above, except reduce mayonnaise or salad dressing to 3 tablespoons and stir in 2 tablespoons purchased pesto.

Per serving (basic B.L.T.): 361 calories, 22 g total fat (5 g saturated), 24 mg cholesterol, 686 mg sodium, 31 g carbohydrate, 4 g fiber, 3 g protein.
Daily Values: 5% vitamin A, 31% vitamin C, 8% calcium, 16% iron.

SNAPPY JOES

On the side, try ice-cold blanched peeled baby carrots or crisp pasta chips. Serve the veggies and chips with this easy, low-fat dip: Beat together equal amounts of light cream cheese (Neufchâtel) and light dairy sour cream. Season with your favorite herb, such as basil, dill, or oregano.

1 pound lean ground beef	½ cup bottled barbecue sauce
½ cup chopped green sweet pepper	1 cup preshredded coleslaw mix
1 small onion, chopped	6 toasted hamburger buns, corn
1 8-ounce can tomato sauce	tortillas, or baked potatoes

1 In a large skillet cook the ground beef, green pepper, and onion for 4 to 5 minutes or till beef no longer is pink. Drain off fat.

2 Stir in the tomato sauce, barbecue sauce, and coleslaw mix. Bring to boiling; reduce heat. Simmer, uncovered, for 10 minutes. Spoon about ½ cup meat mixture onto each bun or over tortillas or potatoes. Makes 6 servings.

Per serving: 277 calories, 8 g total fat (3 g saturated), 43 mg cholesterol, 710 mg sodium, 29 g carbohydrate, 2 g fiber, 21 g protein.
Daily Values: 16% vitamin A, 32% vitamin C, 10% calcium, 18% iron.

FREEZING ONIONS AND SWEET PEPPERS

When you have a spare minute, chop some extra onion or green sweet pepper to use when time is sparse. Spread the chopped onion or sweet pepper in a single layer in a shallow baking pan and place in the freezer until frozen (about an hour). Transfer to freezer bags or containers; then seal, label, and freeze for up to one month. To use, just measure and add to your recipe as if the vegetables were fresh.

QUICK CHICKEN FAJITAS

8 7-inch flour tortillas
12 ounces boneless, skinless chicken
     breasts or turkey tenderloin
     steaks
 1 tablespoon lime juice or lemon juice
 ½ teaspoon ground cumin
 ½ teaspoon ground coriander
 ¼ teaspoon dried oregano, crushed
 ¼ cup clear Italian salad dressing
     (not reduced-oil dressing)

 1 small red and/or green sweet
     pepper, cut into strips
 1 small onion, halved and sliced
     Condiments: salsa, dairy sour
     cream, guacamole, and/or
     jalapeño peppers
     Shredded lettuce (optional)

1 Wrap tortillas in foil; heat in a 350° oven for 10 to 15 minutes or till heated through. Or, wrap in paper towels or waxed paper and heat in a microwave oven on 100% power (high) for 15 to 20 seconds.

2 Thinly slice chicken into bite-size pieces. In a bowl combine lime juice, cumin, coriander, and oregano. Stir in chicken; set aside.

3 In a large skillet heat the salad dressing over medium-high heat. Add chicken mixture. Stir-fry for 2 minutes. With a slotted spoon, remove chicken from skillet. Add sweet pepper and onion to skillet; stir-fry for 2 to 3 minutes or till crisp tender. Return chicken to skillet; heat through.

4 Spoon mixture onto warm tortillas; roll up. Top with favorite condiments. Serve on a bed of shredded lettuce, if desired. Makes 4 servings.

Per serving: 425 calories, 17 g total fat (4 g saturated), 51 mg cholesterol, 600 mg sodium, 45 g carbohydrate, 1 fiber, 23 g protein.
Daily Values: 6% vitamin A, 52% vitamin C, 10% calcium, 22% iron.

After a Tex-Mex meal, serve Almost-Fried Ice Cream: Scoop your favorite ice cream into a shallow pan and place, covered, in the freezer till firm. Stir together 1¼ cups almond cluster multigrain cereal, coarsely crushed, and 2 teaspoons melted margarine. Roll ice cream scoops in cereal mixture; return to freezer till ready to serve. To serve drizzle honey over ice cream and sprinkle with cinnamon.

ORIENTAL TURKEY BURGER

All this burger needs on the side is a fresh spinach salad with a bit of Far East flair. Look in the supermarket produce section for bags of spinach already cleaned and ready for tossing into a bowl. Top with chilled canned mandarin orange sections and a package of broken ramen noodles (but omit the seasoning packet). Serve with poppy seed dressing or your favorite bottled dressing for flavor and to soften the uncooked noodles.

½ cup fine dry bread crumbs	1 tablespoon cooking oil
⅓ cup finely chopped green onion	1 medium carrot, shredded
1 tablespoon soy sauce	1 cup fresh bean sprouts
¼ teaspoon ground ginger	1 tablespoon margarine or butter
¼ teaspoon garlic powder	Soy sauce (optional)
¼ teaspoon bottled hot pepper sauce	Honey mustard (optional)
1 pound ground turkey or chicken	4 hamburger buns, toasted

1 In a bowl combine bread crumbs, green onion, the 1 tablespoon soy sauce, ginger, garlic powder, and hot pepper sauce. Add ground turkey or chicken; mix well. Shape into 4 patties about ¾ inch thick.

2 Heat oil in a 10- or 12-inch skillet. Cook patties in hot oil over medium heat for 10 to 12 minutes or till no longer pink, turning once. Remove burgers from skillet; keep warm.

3 Add shredded carrot, bean sprouts, and margarine or butter to skillet. Cook and stir for 2 to 3 minutes or till carrots are crisp tender. If desired, season vegetables with a few drops of soy sauce. Spread honey mustard on buns, if desired. Place burgers on buns; top with cooked vegetables. Serves 4.

Per serving: 385 calories, 17 g total fat (4 g saturated), 42 mg cholesterol, 682 mg sodium, 35 g carbohydrate, 1 g fiber, 21 g protein.
Daily Values: 44% vitamin A, 11% vitamin C, 8% calcium, 23% iron.

SMOKED TURKEY SALAD SANDWICH

On a hot summer day, this quick sandwich is light and refreshing. Simply pass a serve-yourself relish tray filled with assorted pickles (try some pickled watermelon for a change), crisp cucumber slices, olives, and fresh berries to go with the turkey sandwich.

¼	cup nonfat or regular mayonnaise or salad dressing	
¼	cup plain nonfat yogurt	
½	cup corn relish	
2	cups chopped fully cooked smoked turkey	

1	stalk celery, thinly sliced
4	kaiser rolls, split, or lettuce leaves
1	medium tomato, sliced

1 For dressing, in a small mixing bowl stir together mayonnaise or salad dressing and yogurt. Stir in corn relish.

2 In a large mixing bowl combine turkey and celery. Add dressing; toss gently to coat. Serve on rolls or lettuce leaves with tomato slices. Serves 4.

Per serving: 292 calories, 10 g total fat (1 g saturated), 0 mg cholesterol, 527 sodium, 3 g carbohydrate, 2 g fiber, 18 g protein.
Daily Values: 3% vitamin A, 12% vitamin C, 25% calcium, 16% iron.

SOLE-SLAW SANDWICH

1 to 1¼ pounds fresh or frozen sole
    or flounder fillets, cut into 4
    portions
    Nonstick spray coating
⅓ cup seasoned fine dry bread
    crumbs
⅓ cup grated Parmesan cheese

¼ teaspoon pepper
3 tablespoons all-purpose flour
¼ cup milk
1 cup deli coleslaw
4 multigrain hamburger buns, split
    and toasted

For a picnic-style supper, heat a can of pork and beans, zipped up with a dab or two of mustard. Serve the hot beans and crunchy chips or canned peach slices with the crispy fish sandwiches.

1 Thaw fish, if frozen. (See tip, page 22.) Spray a baking sheet with nonstick coating; set aside.

2 In a shallow bowl or pie plate combine bread crumbs, Parmesan cheese, and pepper. Place flour and milk in two separate shallow bowls or pie plates. Rinse fish and pat dry with paper towels.

3 Fold under ends of fish pieces so each piece is slightly larger than bun. Coat fish with the flour; dip into milk. Then coat completely with crumb mixture. Arrange fillets on prepared baking sheet so they don't touch each other.

4 Bake fish in a 400° oven for 8 to 10 minutes or till fish flakes easily with a fork. Meanwhile, drain excess liquid from coleslaw. Place fish fillets on toasted buns; top with coleslaw. Makes 4 servings.

Per serving: 308 calories, 6 g total fat (3 g saturated), 70 mg cholesterol, 700 mg sodium, 32 g carbohydrate, 3 g fiber, 31 g protein.
Daily Values: 5% vitamin A, 9% vitamin C, 16% calcium, 10% iron.

BLACKENED FISHWICH

The blackened style of cooking fish originated in New Orleans, so a Southern favorite like black-eyed peas makes a great accompaniment to this spicy dish. For a quick side salad with below-the-Mason-Dixon-Line flavor, toss together a can of drained black-eyed peas, sliced celery, sliced green onion, and shredded carrot; finish by adding some bottled Italian salad dressing. Quick-chill the salad by placing it in the freezer for about 10 minutes.

1 pound fresh or frozen cod or
    orange roughy fillets,
    ¾ to 1 inch thick
2 teaspoons Cajun seasoning
2 tablespoons cooking oil

4 leaves leaf lettuce
4 kaiser buns, split and toasted
¼ cup frozen guacamole dip, thawed
1 small tomato, sliced

1 Thaw fish, if frozen. (See tip, page 22.) Rinse fish; pat dry. Cut into 4 serving-size pieces. Rub seasonings onto both sides of fish.

2 In a large skillet heat oil till very hot (a drop of water sizzles in skillet). Carefully cook fish fillets in hot oil over medium heat about 3 minutes on each side or till fish flakes easily with a fork. Place leaf lettuce and fish on bottom half of each toasted bun. Top with guacamole, tomato slices, then bun tops. Makes 4 servings.

Note: If you can't find Cajun seasoning in your supermarket, you can prepare a homemade version. Just stir together ½ teaspoon *onion powder,* ½ teaspoon *garlic powder,* ¼ teaspoon *salt,* ¼ teaspoon *ground thyme,* ¼ teaspoon *ground black pepper,* and ⅛ to ¼ teaspoon *ground red pepper.*

Per serving: 352 calories, 12 g total fat (2 g saturated), 45 mg cholesterol, 711 mg sodium, 35 g carbohydrate, 1 g fiber, 26 g protein.
Daily Values: 9% vitamin A, 13% vitamin C, 7% calcium, 19% iron.

ITALIAN VEGETABLE MELT

2 individual French or Italian loaves, about 6 to 7 inches long

2 tablespoons clear Italian salad dressing

½ small onion, thinly sliced

½ small zucchini, halved lengthwise and sliced

½ small green sweet pepper, cut into thin strips

½ teaspoon bottled minced garlic or 1 clove garlic, minced

1 medium tomato, seeded and chopped

1½ cups shredded provolone or mozzarella cheese (6 ounces)

2 tablespoons grated Parmesan cheese

In summertime, make this garden-fresh sandwich with just-picked vegetables. You might try yellow summer squash, colorful sweet peppers, fennel, or kohlrabi. To keep your dessert cool and carefree, set up a sundae bar. Put out bowls of chopped nuts, fresh fruits, granola, chocolate topping, and whipped cream to spoon over your family's favorite ice cream.

1 Split bread in half horizontally. Place halves on baking sheet, cut side up.

2 In a 10-inch skillet heat the salad dressing. Add onion, zucchini, green pepper, and garlic. Stir-fry for 3 to 5 minutes or till crisp tender. Stir in tomato. Sprinkle half of the provolone or mozzarella cheese on bread halves. Spoon vegetable mixture on cheese; sprinkle with remaining provolone or mozzarella and the Parmesan cheese.

3 Broil 3 to 4 inches from the heat about 2 minutes or till cheese melts. Serve immediately. Makes 4 servings.

Per serving: 374 calories, 18 g total fat (9 g saturated), 32 mg cholesterol, 836 mg sodium, 35 g carbohydrate, 1 g fiber, 18 g protein.
Daily Values: 14% vitamin A, 41% vitamin C, 34% calcium, 13% iron.

CHEESY EGGPLANT-PEPPER CALZONE

Accompany this Italian sandwich with an antipasto-style salad. Drain and chop a jar of marinated artichoke hearts and toss with ripe olives; serve on lettuce leaves.

1 small eggplant*, peeled and cut into ½-inch cubes (4 cups)
1 teaspoon bottled minced garlic or 2 cloves garlic, minced
2 tablespoons cooking oil or olive oil
½ small red sweet pepper*, cut into thin strips
½ teaspoon dried Italian seasoning, crushed
½ teaspoon salt
¼ teaspoon pepper
1 10-ounce package refrigerated pizza dough
2 cups Italian blend shredded cheeses (mozzarella and provolone) or 2 cups shredded mozzarella cheese (8 ounces)
Milk
Grated Parmesan cheese

1 In a large skillet cook the eggplant and garlic in hot oil about 5 minutes or till tender. Stir in sweet pepper strips, Italian seasoning, salt, and pepper. Cook and stir till pepper is just tender. Remove from heat.

2 Unroll pizza dough on an ungreased baking sheet, forming a rectangle. Spread vegetable mixture on half of the dough rectangle, coming to within 1 inch of edges and stopping at middle of rectangle. Sprinkle blended cheeses over vegetables. Moisten edges with water; fold side of dough with no filling over side with filling and seal edge with tines of a fork. Prick top with a fork. Brush with milk; sprinkle with Parmesan cheese.

3 Bake in a 425° oven for 12 to 15 minutes or till golden. Cut into wedges to serve. Makes 4 servings.

*Note: An even faster option is to use 2 cups leftover cooked vegetables in place of the eggplant and sweet pepper. Omit the oil, and sprinkle Italian seasoning over vegetables along with the cheese.

Per serving: 419 calories, 22 g total fat (9 g saturated), 37 mg cholesterol, 906 mg sodium, 35 g carbohydrate, 4 g fiber, 20 g protein.
Daily Values: 22% vitamin A, 38% vitamin C, 36% calcium, 16% iron.

VEGETABLE QUESADILLAS

¾ **cup finely chopped broccoli**
¼ **cup shredded carrot**
¼ **cup sliced green onion**
2 **tablespoons water**
6 **6-inch flour tortillas**
1 **teaspoon cooking oil**

1 **8-ounce package shredded**
  cheddar or Monterey Jack
  cheese with jalapeño peppers
Dairy sour cream (optional)
Salsa (optional)
Sliced pitted ripe olives (optional)
Sliced green onion (optional)

Mix together a Mock Tequila Sunrise to go along with the Southwest flavors of the quesadilla. In a small pitcher combine 2 cups orange juice, 1 cup apricot nectar, and 3 tablespoons lemon juice. Pour over ice in glasses. Slowly add 1 to 2 teaspoons grenadine syrup to each glass, then stir. Garnish with lime wedges.

1 In a 1-quart microwave-safe casserole combine the broccoli, carrot, green onion, and water. Micro-cook, covered, on 100% power (high) for 2 to 4 minutes or till vegetables are crisp-tender. Drain.

2 Brush one side of 3 tortillas with some of the oil. Place tortillas, oiled side down, on a baking sheet. Top with the cheese, vegetable mixture, and remaining tortillas. Brush tops with remaining oil. Bake in a 450° oven about 6 minutes or till light brown.

3 To serve, cut each tortilla into wedges. Serve with sour cream, salsa, olives, and green onion, if desired. Makes 3 servings.

Per serving: 499 calories, 30 g total fat (17 g saturated), 80 mg cholesterol, 728 mg sodium, 32 g carbohydrate, 1 g fiber, 24 g protein.
Daily Values: 54% vitamin A, 38% vitamin C, 52% calcium, and 16% iron.

CURRIED ROAST BEEF SANDWICH

A pasta salad side dish comes together quickly if you remember to always cook extra pasta when you fix it for dinner. Store cooked pasta in your refrigerator for 4 to 5 days. Toss it with a bottled dressing and any chopped vegetables for a high-carbohydrate accompaniment to the sandwich.

¼ cup mayonnaise or salad dressing
2 tablespoons chutney, chopped
½ teaspoon curry powder
¼ cup chunky peanut butter
8 slices whole grain bread or
  rye bread

½ pound thinly sliced, cooked lean
  roast beef or pork*
8 thin slices tomato
4 lettuce leaves

1 In a bowl stir together the mayonnaise or salad dressing, chutney, and curry powder; set aside.

2 Spread peanut butter on four of the bread slices. Top with roast beef or pork. Spoon curry mixture on meat; top with tomato, lettuce, and remaining slices of bread. Makes 4 servings.

*Note: You can use leftover roast beef or pork in the sandwich instead of the deli slices. Chop the roast into bite-size pieces and combine with some of the mayonnaise mixture before assembling sandwiches. If desired, use the sandwich filling in pita bread halves. Concerned about fat? Use nonfat mayonnaise or salad dressing.

Per serving: 467 calories, 25 g total fat (5 g saturated), 53 mg cholesterol, 487 mg sodium, 37 g carbohydrate, 5 g fiber, 28 g protein.
Daily Values: 3% vitamin A, 11% vitamin C, 9% calcium, 26% iron.

STIR-FRIED CHICKEN PIZZA

1 10-ounce package refrigerated pizza dough
3 medium skinless, boneless chicken breast halves (about 9 ounces total)
1 tablespoon cooking oil or olive oil
1 large onion, sliced and separated into rings
1 medium green or red sweet pepper, chopped

1 cup sliced fresh mushrooms
1 teaspoon bottled minced garlic or 2 cloves garlic, minced
1½ cups shredded mozzarella cheese (6 ounces)
1 tablespoon snipped fresh basil or ½ teaspoon dried basil, crushed
1 teaspoon sesame seeds (optional)

Your kids will love it when you announce that pizza and pop are for supper. And you can feel good about serving this homemade version of soda pop: Stir together a 6-ounce can of their favorite frozen juice concentrate (orange, apple, or grape) with 3 juice cans filled with carbonated water (18 ounces water total). Serve over ice.

1 Unroll pizza dough; pat into a greased 12-inch pizza pan. Bake in a 425° oven for 8 minutes. Meanwhile, rinse chicken and pat dry; cut chicken into thin bite-size strips and set aside.

2 In a large skillet heat oil. Stir-fry the onion, pepper, mushrooms, and garlic over high heat for 2 to 3 minutes or till crisp tender. Remove from skillet.

3 Stir-fry chicken for 2 to 3 minutes or till no longer pink (add more oil, if necessary, during cooking). Return vegetables to skillet; toss to mix and heat through.

4 Sprinkle half of the cheese over pizza crust. Spoon chicken mixture evenly over cheese layer. Top with remaining cheese. Sprinkle with basil and, if desired, sesame seeds. Return to 425° oven for 5 to 7 minutes more or till cheese melts. Makes 4 servings.

Per serving: 385 calories, 15 g total fat (6 g saturated), 57 mg cholesterol, 457 mg sodium, 34 g carbohydrate, 2 g fiber, 28 g protein.
Daily Values: 8% vitamin A, 26% vitamin C, 25% calcium, 17% iron.

CINNAMON CHICKEN SALAD

Before stirring together this main-dish salad, put a quick batch of refrigerated crescent dough in the oven. Serve the crescents with honey butter. Pour yourself a tall glass of iced tea to go with the refreshing salad and warm bread.

2 cups cooked, cubed chicken or turkey or two 5-ounce cans chunk-style chicken, drained and flaked
1 cup seedless grapes, halved
½ cup sliced celery
½ cup chopped cucumber
½ cup toasted chopped walnuts or pecans
⅓ cup plain low-fat yogurt
⅓ cup mayonnaise or salad dressing
½ teaspoon ground cinnamon
⅛ teaspoon salt
⅛ teaspoon pepper
Spinach and/or curly endive or lettuce leaves

1 In a large bowl combine chicken, grapes, celery, cucumber, and walnuts.

2 For dressing, combine yogurt, mayonnaise or salad dressing, cinnamon, salt, and pepper; mix well.

3 Add dressing to salad; toss to coat. Serve on spinach or lettuce leaves. Makes 4 servings.

Per serving: 423 calories, 30 g total fat (5 g saturated), 80 mg cholesterol, 275 mg sodium, 13 g carbohydrate, 2 g fiber, 26 g protein.
Daily Values: 13% vitamin A, 17% vitamin C, 7% calcium, 14% iron.

EASY POPCORN SNACKS

When you're looking for a quick between-meal snack or party appetizer, toss together one of these ideas. Each starts with 4 cups popped popcorn.
■ Toss popcorn and 2 cups oyster crackers with 3 tablespoons melted margarine. Sprinkle with 1 tablespoon dry buttermilk salad dressing mix; toss.
■ Stir together 2 tablespoons melted margarine and 1 teaspoon dried Italian seasoning, crushed. Drizzle over popcorn.
■ Toss popcorn with 2 tablespoons melted margarine. Sprinkle with 3 table-spoons dry regular or instant chocolate or butterscotch pudding mix; toss.
■ Toss popcorn with 2 tablespoons melted margarine. Sprinkle with 2 table-spoons grated Parmesan cheese and 1 teaspoon chili powder; toss.
■ Toss popcorn with 2 tablespoons melted margarine. Sprinkle with ½ tea-spoon ground cinnamon; toss to coat. Stir in ¾ cup candy-coated milk chocolate pieces and ¾ cup cashews or peanuts.

SO-EASY COOKING

Gives You Time to Yourself

When you seek some leisure time before dinner, fix an oven meal, soup, stew, or crockery cooker recipe from this chapter. Each goes together quickly, then simmers slowly and easily—with little or no peeking into the pot. Wind down from work, discuss your family's day, steal a few quiet moments in the garden, or chat with a neighbor. Remember, time is on your side when you prepare any of these recipes. So, go ahead and linger—these are dinners that wait for you.

Look for this symbol—it denotes recipes for crockery cookers.

APRICOT CHICKEN

Bake a no-fuss vegetable, such as acorn squash, with the chicken as it cooks. Wash a medium squash (about 1 pound); halve and remove seeds. Place halves, cut side down, in a baking dish. Bake in the 375° oven for 30 minutes. Turn cut side up, cover, and bake 20 to 25 minutes more or till tender. Drizzle with melted margarine or butter and a sprinkle of nutmeg before serving.

Prep: 10 minutes
Cook: 45 to 50 minutes

2 **pounds meaty chicken pieces**	⅓ **cup apricot jam, large pieces cut up**
Salt and pepper to taste	1½ **teaspoons ground cumin**
⅓ **cup plain yogurt**	

1 Remove skin from chicken, if desired. Rinse chicken; pat dry with paper towels. Arrange chicken pieces in a 3-quart rectangular baking pan, skin side up, so pieces do not touch. Sprinkle lightly with salt and pepper.

2 Bake, uncovered, in a 375° oven for 40 minutes. Drain off any fat from pan.

3 Meanwhile, stir together the yogurt, apricot jam, and cumin. Spoon yogurt mixture over chicken. Bake for 5 to 10 minutes more or till chicken is tender and no longer pink. Makes 4 servings.

Per serving (with skin): 351 calories, 14 g total fat (4 g saturated), 106 mg cholesterol, 176 mg sodium, 21 g carbohydrate, 0 g fiber, 35 g protein.
Daily Values: 4% vitamin A, 0% vitamin C, 5% calcium, 18% iron.

RECIPE TIME ESTIMATES

The timings listed for each recipe should be used only as general guidelines. Some cooks will work faster and others will work slower than the times given. Here are some other points to remember when referring to these timings:

■ Preparation timings have been rounded to the nearest 5 minute increments.

■ Timings assume some steps can be performed simultaneously. For example, vegetables may be cut up while the water for pasta comes to a boil.

■ Listings include the time to chop, slice, or otherwise prepare ingredients (such as cooking rice when a recipe calls for cooked rice).

■ When a recipe gives an ingredient substitution, calculations were made using the first ingredient.

■ Cooking done as part of the preparation of the recipe is counted as preparation time.

■ When a recipe gives alternate cooking methods, timings refer to the first method.

■ The preparation of optional ingredients is not included.

CRANBERRY CHICKEN

1 8-ounce can whole cranberry sauce
½ cup Russian salad dressing
1 tablespoon dried minced onion
½ teaspoon garlic salt
¼ teaspoon pepper
2 pounds meaty chicken pieces

1 In a mixing bowl stir together the cranberry sauce, salad dressing, onion, garlic salt, and pepper.

2 Remove skin from chicken, if desired. Rinse chicken; pat dry with paper towels. Place chicken pieces in a 3-quart rectangular baking dish. Pour cranberry mixture over chicken.

3 Bake, uncovered, in a 350° oven for 45 to 50 minutes or till chicken is tender and no longer pink. Transfer chicken to platter; skim fat from pan juices. Spoon juices over chicken. Makes 4 servings.

Per serving (with skin): 499 calories, 28 g total fat (6 g saturated), 104 mg cholesterol, 630 mg sodium, 27 g carbohydrate, 1 g fiber, 34 g protein.
Daily Values: 10% vitamin A, 8% vitamin C, 2% calcium, 11% iron.

Regardless of the season, you can enjoy the flavors of a Thanksgiving feast in this easygoing meal made from ingredients probably kept on hand. While the chicken bakes, fix enough stuffing mix for four servings. In your microwave oven, cook 2 cups fresh or frozen brussels sprouts, then toss with margarine or butter, a tablespoon of frozen orange juice concentrate (thawed), and ¼ teaspoon ground ginger. The result? A meal so easy and so delicious you'll be thankful every day of the year.

Prep: 10 minutes
Bake: 45 to 50 minutes

FRENCH-GLAZED CHICKEN

After placing the chicken in the oven, relax about 45 minutes before putting together the finishing touches for this off-the-shelf meal. In a 1½-quart microwave-safe casserole place ½ pound new potatoes, quartered, and ½ pound baby carrots with 2 tablespoons water. Cover and micro-cook on 100% power (high) for 12 to 14 minutes or till potatoes are tender, stirring twice. Dot with margarine or butter and snipped parsley before serving.

Prep: 10 minutes
Bake: 50 to 60 minutes

2 **pounds meaty chicken pieces**
¼ **cup French salad dressing**
2 **tablespoons peach jam, large pieces cut up**

1 **tablespoon water**
1 **teaspoon dried minced onion or 2 tablespoons finely chopped onion**

1 Remove skin from chicken, if desired. Rinse chicken; pat dry with paper towels. Place chicken pieces in a 3 quart-rectangular baking pan.

2 For glaze, stir together the salad dressing, peach jam, water, and onion. Brush the glaze lightly over the chicken.

3 Bake, uncovered, in a 375° oven for 45 to 55 minutes or till chicken is tender and no longer pink. Brush with remaining glaze; bake 5 minutes more. Makes 4 servings.

Per serving (with skin): 353 calories, 19 g total fat (5 g saturated), 106 mg cholesterol, 306 mg sodium, 10 g carbohydrate, 0 g fiber, 34 g protein.
Daily Values: 4% vitamin A, 0% vitamin C, 1% calcium, 10% iron.

OVEN-FRIED HERB CHICKEN

You can easily satisfy a craving for crispy chicken; just make a double or triple batch of the seasoned crumb mixture and store in a covered container until needed. Use ⅔ cup crumb mixture for 2½ to 3 pounds of chicken pieces and coat as directed above. It's also great for oven-fried fish: Use a 425° oven, and allow 4 to 6 minutes baking time per half-inch thickness of fish. While your chicken or fish bakes, cook scalloped potato mix alongside your entrée. Top off your meal with already-prepared corn relish—heated or not, the choice is yours.

Prep: 15 minutes
Bake: 40 to 50 minutes

2½ **to 3 pounds meaty chicken pieces**	½ **teaspoon poultry seasoning**
⅔ **cup cornflake crumbs**	½ **teaspoon dried basil, crushed**
1 **teaspoon paprika**	½ **teaspoon dried oregano, crushed**
¾ **teaspoon garlic salt or onion salt**	¼ **teaspoon pepper**

1 Remove skin from chicken, if desired. Rinse chicken, but don't pat dry.

2 In a plastic bag or a bowl combine cornflake crumbs, paprika, garlic salt or onion salt, poultry seasoning, basil, oregano, and pepper. Place chicken pieces, one or two at a time, in the crumb mixture. Shake or turn to coat evenly. Place chicken pieces, skin side up, on a rack in a shallow baking pan so pieces do not touch.

3 Bake, uncovered, in a 375° oven for 40 to 50 minutes or till chicken is tender and no longer pink. Do not turn during cooking. Makes 6 servings.

Per serving (with skin): 236 calories, 11 g total fat (3 g saturated), 86 mg cholesterol, 395 mg sodium, 5 g carbohydrate, 0 g fiber, 28 g protein.
Daily Values: 12% vitamin A, 5% vitamin C, 1% calcium, 11% iron.

FILIPINO CHICKEN

8 chicken thighs (about 2 pounds)
1 tablespoon cooking oil or olive oil
⅓ cup water
¼ cup white vinegar
¼ cup soy sauce
2 bay leaves

1 teaspoon bottled minced garlic or
   2 cloves garlic, minced
¼ teaspoon pepper
2 tablespoons sliced fresh red chili
   pepper or ¼ cup toasted
   shredded coconut (optional)

1 Remove skin from chicken. Rinse chicken; pat dry with paper towels. In a 10-inch skillet brown chicken thighs on all sides in hot oil. Drain off fat.

2 Add water, vinegar, soy sauce, bay leaves, garlic, and pepper to skillet; stir gently. Bring to boiling; reduce heat. Cover and simmer for 30 to 35 minutes or till chicken is tender and no longer pink. Transfer chicken to a platter; keep warm.

3 Bring liquid in skillet to boiling; boil, uncovered, for 3 to 5 minutes or till reduced to about ½ cup. Skim off fat. Remove and discard bay leaves. Drizzle juices over chicken. Sprinkle with chili pepper or coconut, if desired. Makes 4 servings.

Per serving: 257 calories, 14 g total fat (5 g saturated), 93 mg cholesterol, 1,006 mg sodium, 5 g carbohydrate, 0 g fiber, 27 g protein.
Daily Values: 1% vitamin A, 1% vitamin C, 1% calcium, 12% iron.

While the chicken bakes, cut up and cook about a pound of fresh broccoli till crisp-tender. Drain. Stir together 1 tablespoon soy sauce, 1 teaspoon sesame seeds, and a sprinkling of sesame oil; toss with hot cooked broccoli. Serve with hot cooked rice, if desired, to complete your meal of Far East enchantment.

Prep: 15 minutes
Cook: 35 to 40 minutes

SO-EASY COOKING CHICKEN

ROSEMARY CHICKEN WITH PASTA

You'll love the aroma of this steaming meal when you walk through your door after being away for the afternoon. As the meal finishes cooking, toss together a spinach salad with blue cheese crumbles, croutons, and Italian salad dressing. Bake a batch of brown-and-serve rolls, too, if you worked up an extra-hearty appetite while away from home.

Prep: 15 minutes
Cook: 3½ to 7 hours

2 medium onions, sliced or chopped
2 teaspoons bottled minced garlic or 4 cloves garlic, minced
12 ounces skinless, boneless chicken breasts or thighs
1 16-ounce can diced tomatoes
1 6-ounce can tomato paste
2 tablespoons wine vinegar
2 bay leaves
1 teaspoon sugar
½ teaspoon dried rosemary, crushed
¼ teaspoon salt
¼ teaspoon pepper
1 4-ounce can sliced mushrooms, drained
8 ounces pasta such as penne, mostaccioli, or elbow macaroni
Grated Parmesan cheese

1 In a 3½- to 4½-quart crockery cooker place the onion and garlic. Rinse chicken; pat dry with paper towels. Add chicken to cooker.

2 In a mixing bowl combine undrained tomatoes, tomato paste, vinegar, bay leaves, sugar, rosemary, salt, and pepper; mix well. Pour over chicken.

3 Cover and cook on low-heat setting for 7 hours or on high-heat setting for 3½ hours.

4 When ready to serve, remove bay leaves. Stir mushrooms into chicken mixture; cook for 5 to 10 minutes more to heat through. Meanwhile, cook pasta according to package directions. Serve the chicken and sauce over the hot cooked pasta; sprinkle with Parmesan cheese. Makes 4 servings.

Per serving: 415 calories, 5 g total fat (2 g saturated), 47 mg cholesterol, 568 mg sodium, 65 g carbohydrate, 4 g fiber, 29 g protein.
Daily Values: 18% vitamin A, 63% vitamin C, 10% calcium, 35% iron.

CROCKERY COOKERS VERSUS SLOW COOKERS

The recipes in this book were tested in crockery cookers, not slow cookers. A crockery cooker is a ceramic chamber that heats from the sides, but not the bottom; a slow cooker is a covered casserole that sits on a heated platform. A crockery cooker lets you cook at one of two heat settings—low or high—but a slow cooker has up to five settings. If you have a slow cooker, the timings in our crockery cooker recipes will be too long, so you'll need to adjust them a bit.

TURKEY LOAF WITH PESTO

1 egg, beaten
¾ cup soft rye bread crumbs (1 slice)
¾ cup shredded provolone or
    mozzarella cheese (3 ounces)
3 tablespoons beer, milk, or water
2 tablespoons purchased pesto

¼ teaspoon ground nutmeg
¼ teaspoon pepper
1 pound ground turkey
    Shredded provolone or mozzarella
    (optional)

1 In a large bowl combine egg, bread crumbs, the ¾ cup cheese, desired liquid, pesto, nutmeg, and pepper. Add turkey; mix well. Form into a loaf and place in an 8x4x3-inch loaf pan.

2 Bake in a 350° oven for 45 to 50 minutes or till meat no longer is pink.

3 Remove from oven. Transfer loaf to a platter; top with additional cheese, if desired. Let stand 5 minutes before slicing. Makes 4 servings.

Note: In summer, when you don't want to turn on your oven, make this meat loaf in your crockery cooker. Cover and cook on low-heat setting for 8 to 10 hours or on high-heat setting for 4 to 5 hours. To make lifting the meat loaf into and out of the cooker easy, use foil strips. Form 3 long strips of folded foil and place them in a spoke design under center of the uncooked loaf. Lift the ends of the foil strips and transfer the meat to the crockery cooker. Leave the strips under the meat during cooking, then use strips to lift the loaf out of cooker when the meat is done.

Per serving: 315 calories, 21 g total fat (6 g saturated), 111 mg cholesterol, 364 mg sodium, 6 g carbohydrate, 0 g fiber, 24 g protein.
Daily Values: 7% vitamin A, 0% vitamin C, 15% calcium, 11% iron.

While the loaf bakes, you'll have time to make real mashed potatoes, but keep it easy by keeping the potato skins on.

Boil the chopped potatoes (along with a quartered onion or chopped garlic cloves) till tender. Drain and mash. The potato skins add flavor and fiber, and the onion or garlic turn plain mashed potatoes into a tasty treat.

Prep: 15 minutes
Bake: 45 to 50 minutes

INDONESIAN-STYLE ROUND STEAK

To temper the curry-flavored edge of the meat and gravy, try a platter of refreshing in-season fruits. For color and texture, use a variety of fruits such as cherries, pineapple wedges, and sliced mango, papaya, kiwi fruit, star fruit, and apricots.

Prep: 15 minutes
Cook: 1 to 1¼ hours

1 pound boneless beef round steak or chuck steak, cut ¾ to 1 inch thick
1 tablespoon olive oil or cooking oil
1½ cups water
1 medium onion, chopped
¼ cup chutney, snipped
¼ cup raisins
2 teaspoons instant beef bouillon granules

1½ to 2 teaspoons curry powder
¼ teaspoon garlic powder
¼ teaspoon ground ginger
1 cup long grain rice
Snipped parsley (optional)
Chopped peanuts (optional)
1 tablespoon cornstarch

1 Cut steak into four serving-size pieces. Trim off any separable fat. In a 10-inch skillet brown steak on all sides in hot oil (about 8 to 10 minutes). Drain off any fat.

2 Add 1 cup of the water to skillet along with onion, chutney, raisins, bouillon granules, curry powder, garlic powder, and ginger. Bring to boiling; reduce heat. Cover and simmer for 1 to 1¼ hours.

3 Meanwhile, cook rice according to package directions. If desired, stir some snipped parsley and chopped peanuts into the cooked rice; keep warm.

4 Remove meat to platter; keep warm. For gravy, combine remaining ½ cup water and the cornstarch; stir cornstarch mixture into skillet. Cook and stir over medium heat till thickened and bubbly. Cook and stir for 2 minutes more. Serve steak with rice and curry gravy; sprinkle with more peanuts, if desired. Makes 4 servings.

Per serving: 444 calories, 10 g total fat (3 g saturated), 72 mg cholesterol, 500 mg sodium, 55 g carbohydrate, 4 g fiber, 32 g protein.
Daily Values: 1% vitamin A, 3% vitamin C, 3% calcium, 24% iron.

BEEF BRISKET WITH BEER AND ONIONS

1 3½-pound fresh beef brisket, trimmed of fat
2 large onions, sliced and separated into rings
1 large red sweet pepper, sliced into rings
1 12-ounce can beer
¾ cup chili sauce
3 tablespoons brown sugar

1 tablespoon prepared horseradish
1 teaspoon bottled minced garlic or 2 cloves garlic, minced
1 teaspoon salt
½ teaspoon pepper
½ cup water
¼ cup all-purpose flour

1 Place brisket in a 3-quart rectangular baking dish. Top with onion and sweet pepper.

2 In a bowl combine beer, chili sauce, brown sugar, horseradish, garlic, salt, and pepper; pour over meat. Cover dish tightly with foil.

3 Bake in a 350° oven about 3½ hours or till meat is tender. Remove meat and vegetables to a platter; keep warm.

4 Pour 2¼ cups of the cooking liquid into a saucepan; bring to boiling. Stir together water and flour till well blended; stir into saucepan mixture. Cook and stir over medium heat till thickened and bubbly. Cook and stir for 1 minute more. Thinly slice brisket across the grain; serve with gravy. Makes 10 servings.

Per serving: 355 calories, 15 g total fat (5 g saturated), 109 mg cholesterol, 561 mg sodium, 15 g carbohydrate, 1 g fiber, 36 g protein.
Daily Values: 8% vitamin A, 27% vitamin C, 2% calcium, 24% iron.

You can also prepare this long-cooking meat in a crockery cooker. Place onion and sweet pepper in the bottom of a 3½- to 6-quart cooker, then top with the brisket. Combine sauce ingredients and pour over meat. Cover and cook on low-heat setting for 10 to 12 hours or on high-heat setting for 5 to 6 hours. Remove meat and vegetables to a platter; keep warm. Prepare gravy as directed in the recipe.

The night before serving, you can layer the meat, vegetables, and sauce in the baking dish or in your crockery cooker if it has a removable liner; cover, then chill overnight or up to 24 hours. For a no-fuss zesty side dish, buy a pint of three-bean salad.

Prep: 30 minutes
Bake: 3½ hours

SWISS STEAK CAFÉ

This long-simmering entrée will fill your home with an enchanting fragrance. But, before succumbing to its magical spell, fix a saucepanful of quick-cooking brown rice to round out the meal. For added flavor and color, stir in shredded carrot and frozen baby peas during the last 5 minutes the rice cooks.

Prep: 20 minutes
Cook: 4 to 10 hours

1½ **pounds boneless beef round steak,
    cut ¾ inch thick**
 1 **tablespoon olive oil or cooking oil**
 2 **onions, sliced**
 1 **cup strong coffee**
 2 **tablespoons soy sauce**

 1 **teaspoon bottled minced garlic or
    2 cloves garlic, minced**
 2 **bay leaves**
 ½ **teaspoon dried oregano, crushed**
 2 **tablespoons water**
 4 **teaspoons cornstarch**

1 Trim separable fat from meat; cut meat into four serving-size pieces. In a 12-inch skillet brown meat on all sides in hot oil. Drain off fat.

2 Place onion in the bottom of a 3½- to 6-quart crockery cooker. Add meat. Combine coffee, soy sauce, garlic, bay leaves, and oregano; pour over meat and onion.

3 Cover and cook on low-heat setting for 8 to 10 hours or on high-heat setting for 4 to 5 hours.

4 Remove meat and onions to platter; keep warm. Measure 2 cups cooking juices; pour into a small saucepan. Discard bay leaves. Combine water and cornstarch; stir into saucepan. Cook and stir over medium heat till thickened and bubbly. Cook and stir for 2 minutes more. Serve sauce with round steak. Makes 6 servings.

Per serving: 208 calories, 8 g total fat (2 g saturated), 72 mg cholesterol, 360 mg sodium, 5 g carbohydrate, 0 g fiber, 28 g protein.
Daily Values: 0% vitamin A, 2% vitamin C, 1% calcium, 18% iron.

CAJUN POT ROAST

1 2- to 2½ -pound boneless beef
  chuck pot roast
2 to 3 teaspoons Cajun seasoning*
1 tablespoon cooking oil
1 14½-ounce can Cajun-style or
  Mexican-style stewed tomatoes

1 cup chopped onion
1 cup chopped celery
¼ cup quick-cooking tapioca
1 teaspoon bottled minced garlic or
  2 cloves garlic, minced
  Hot cooked rice

1 Trim fat from roast. Cut roast to fit in crockery cooker, if necessary. Rub Cajun seasoning all over meat. In a large skillet brown meat on all sides in hot oil.

2 In a 3½- to 4-quart crockery cooker combine undrained tomatoes, onion, celery, tapioca, and garlic. Place meat on top of vegetable mixture.

3 Cover and cook on low-heat setting for 10 to 12 hours or on high-heat setting for 5 to 6 hours.

4 Slice meat; serve with sauce over rice. Makes 6 servings.

*Note: Look for Cajun seasoning in the spice section of your supermarket. Or, to make your own, mix together 1 to 1½ teaspoons *seasoned salt,* ½ to ¾ teaspoon *ground red pepper,* and ½ to ¾ teaspoon *ground black pepper.*

Note: This mildly spiced meat and sauce also makes a delicious hot sandwich. Using two forks, shred any leftover meat. Combine the shredded beef and remaining sauce in a storage container; cover and freeze for up to 3 months. When ready to eat, thaw mixture overnight in the refrigerator. Pour into a saucepan and heat through. Serve on hard rolls with sliced tomato and sliced green onion.

Per serving: 273 calories, 7 g total fat (2 g saturated), 55 mg cholesterol, 366 mg sodium, 31 g carbohydrate, 2 g fiber, 21 g protein.
Daily Values: 8% vitamin A, 19% vitamin C, 4% calcium, 20% iron.

In Cajun country (southern Louisiana), okra is a mainstay item. This small green (or purple) edible pod has a fuzzy ridged skin. If you can't find it fresh, look for it in the frozen food section. Cook fresh whole okra in a small amount of boiling water for 8 to 15 minutes or till tender. Cook frozen okra according to package directions. Fresh or frozen okra is the classic choice for this meal.

Prep: 25 minutes
Cook: 5 to 12 hours

GINGER AND MOLASSES BEEF STEW

You can avoid an early-morning rush by doing some of the food prep the night before. Brown the meat, drain well, wrap in foil, and chill. Then clean, chop, and store vegetables in the refrigerator in an airtight container. Combine the tomato sauce ingredients in a bowl and chill, covered. The next morning, combine the ingredients in the crockery cooker as directed in the recipe.

After stirring the raisins into the hot pot, heat up your oven to bake a package of refrigerated biscuit dough.

Prep: 35 minutes
Cook: 4½ to 10½ hours

2 **pounds lean beef stew meat, cut into 1-inch pieces**	¼ **cup quick-cooking tapioca**
1 **tablespoon cooking oil**	1 **16-ounce can diced tomatoes**
4 **carrots, sliced**	¼ **cup vinegar**
2 **medium parsnips, sliced**	¼ **cup molasses**
1 **large onion, sliced**	1 **teaspoon salt**
1 **stalk celery, sliced**	½ **teaspoon pepper**
1 **¼-inch slice fresh gingerroot or ½ teaspoon ground ginger**	½ **cup raisins**

1 In a 10-inch skillet brown the meat, a third at a time, in hot oil. Drain off any fat.

2 In a 3½- to 6-quart crockery cooker place carrots, parsnips, onion, celery, and gingerroot (if using). Sprinkle tapioca over vegetables. Place meat in cooker. Combine undrained tomatoes, vinegar, molasses, salt, pepper, and ground ginger (if using); pour over meat.

3 Cover and cook on low-heat setting for 9 to 10 hours or on high-heat setting for 4 to 5 hours.

4 Stir in raisins; cover and cook for 30 minutes more.

5 Remove slice of gingerroot (if used) before serving. Makes 6 to 8 servings.

Per serving: 564 calories, 19 g total fat (5 g saturated), 110 mg cholesterol, 962 mg sodium, 58 mg carbohydrate, 4 g fiber, 40 g protein.
Daily Values: 119% vitamin A, 29% vitamin C, 9% calcium, 48% iron.

BEEF BURGUNDY

You can use an automatic timer to start the cooker while you're away from home. The food, however, should not stand more than two hours before the cooker comes on. First, assemble the recipe and thoroughly chill it. (You can do this the night before.) When it's time to leave your house, place the food in the cooker. Plug the cooker into the timer, set the timer, and turn on the cooker. Dinner's ready when you are!

Prep: 20 minutes
Cook: 4 to 10 hours

1 10¾-ounce can condensed golden mushroom soup
¾ cup burgundy
¼ cup quick-cooking tapioca
1 teaspoon dried thyme, crushed
¼ teaspoon pepper
3 medium carrots, cut into 1-inch pieces
1 large onion, cut into thin wedges
1½ pounds lean beef stew meat, cut into ¾-inch cubes
8 ounces fresh mushrooms, halved
  Hot cooked noodles

1 In a 3½- to 6-quart crockery cooker stir together the soup, burgundy, tapioca, thyme, and pepper. Add the carrots and onion. Top with the stew meat and mushrooms.

2 Cover and cook on low-heat setting for 8 to 10 hours or on high-heat setting for 4 to 5 hours.

3 Serve over hot cooked noodles. Makes 6 servings.

Per serving: 402 calories, 10 g total fat (4 g saturated), 83 mg cholesterol, 488 mg sodium, 41 g carbohydrate, 2 g fiber, 32 g protein.
Daily Values: 92% vitamin A, 6% vitamin C, 3% calcium, 37% iron.

MEDITERRANEAN BEEF STEW

- 2 pounds boneless beef chuck pot roast, cut into ¾-inch cubes
- 1 to 2 tablespoons olive oil
- 2 cups beef broth
- 1 16-ounce can diced tomatoes
- ¼ cup quick-cooking tapioca
- ¼ cup balsamic vinegar or red wine vinegar
- 1 tablespoon honey
- 2 teaspoons ground cinnamon
- ¼ teaspoon garlic powder

- ¼ teaspoon pepper
- 2 medium onions, cut into thin wedges, or one 16-ounce package frozen small white onions
- 3 cups peeled sweet potato or butternut squash cubes
- 2 cups pitted prunes
  Hot cooked couscous or brown rice

1 In a 4½-quart Dutch oven brown meat cubes, a third at a time, in 1 tablespoon hot oil, adding more oil if necessary. Drain off any fat. Return all meat to Dutch oven. Stir in the broth, undrained tomatoes, tapioca, vinegar, honey, cinnamon, garlic powder, and pepper. Bring to boiling; reduce heat.

2 Cover and simmer for 1 hour, stirring occasionally. Stir in the onions and sweet potato or squash; cook, covered, for 20 to 30 minutes more or till meat and vegetables are tender.

3 Stir in prunes; heat through. Serve over couscous or rice. Makes 8 servings.

Per serving: 495 calories, 11 g total fat (4 g saturated), 82 mg cholesterol, 452 mg sodium, 67 g carbohydrate, 9 g fiber, 34 g protein.
Daily Values: 107% vitamin A, 38% vitamin C, 6% calcium, 38% iron.

Almost any long-simmering mixture can be prepared in a crockery cooker following these simple steps: First, brown the meat and drain; set aside. Place uncooked vegetables and the seasonings in the bottom of the crockery cooker. Place the meat on top and pour on any sauce. This allows the vegetables to cook till tender without overcooking the meat. Depending on the quantity of food and type of meat cut, the dish can be ready in 5 to 10 hours on low-heat setting. Check your dish frequently to test for doneness the first time you adjust a recipe to a crockery cooker.

Prep: 35 minutes
Cook: 1⅓ to 1½ hours

CINCINNATI-STYLE CHILI

A stocked freezer is a busy cook's best friend, and this recipe is ideal for making ahead. Prepare the recipe as directed, then cool. Freeze the mixture in two 1-quart freezer containers. To reheat one portion, transfer the chili to a medium bowl or microwave-safe casserole. Micro-cook, covered, on 70% power (medium-high) for 20 to 25 minutes or till heated through, stirring occasionally.

Prep: 20 minutes
Cook: 45 minutes

1½ pounds lean ground beef
2 large onions, chopped
3 8-ounce cans tomato sauce
1 cup water
½ ounce unsweetened chocolate, cut up
2 tablespoons chili powder
2 tablespoons vinegar
2 teaspoons Worcestershire sauce
1½ teaspoons ground cinnamon
1 teaspoon ground cumin
½ teaspoon salt

¼ teaspoon garlic powder
¼ teaspoon ground allspice
⅛ teaspoon ground cloves
1 bay leaf
1 dried red chili pepper or
  ¼ teaspoon ground red pepper
  Hot cooked spaghetti
  Chopped onion (optional)
  Shredded cheddar cheese (optional)
1 15-ounce can kidney beans,
  warmed and drained (optional)

1 In a 4½-quart Dutch oven cook ground beef and the 2 chopped onions till beef no longer is pink. Drain off any fat.

2 Add the tomato sauce, water, chocolate, chili powder, vinegar, Worcestershire sauce, cinnamon, cumin, salt, garlic powder, allspice, clove, bay leaf, and red chili pepper or ground red pepper. Bring to boiling; reduce heat. Simmer, covered, over low heat for 45 minutes or till desired consistency, stirring once or twice.

3 Remove bay leaf and, if using, chili pepper. Serve over spaghetti and, if desired, top with onion, cheese, and/or beans. Makes 8 servings.

Per serving: 327 calories, 13 g total fat (5 g saturated), 52 mg cholesterol, 733 mg sodium, 33 g carbohydrate, 4 g fiber, 20 g protein.
Daily Values: 16% vitamin A, 18% vitamin C, 4% calcium, 28% iron.

BAVARIAN PORK ROAST

1 1½- to 2-pound boneless pork
   shoulder roast
2 teaspoons caraway seed
1 teaspoon dried marjoram, crushed
¾ teaspoon salt
½ teaspoon pepper

1 tablespoon olive oil or cooking oil
½ cup water
2 tablespoons white wine vinegar
1 8-ounce carton dairy sour cream or
   plain yogurt
4 teaspoons cornstarch

1 Trim fat from roast. If necessary, cut roast to fit into a 3½- to 6-quart crockery cooker. Combine caraway seed, marjoram, salt, and pepper. Rub all over roast.

2 In a large skillet, brown pork roast on all sides in hot oil. Drain off fat. Place meat in crockery cooker. Add the water to skillet; bring to a gentle boil over medium heat, stirring to loosen brown bits in bottom of skillet. Pour skillet juices and vinegar into crockery cooker.

3 Cover and cook on low-heat setting for 8 to 10 hours or on high-heat setting for 4 to 5 hours. Remove meat from cooker; keep warm.

4 For gravy, skim fat from juices; measure 1¼ cups juices (add water, if necessary). Pour juices into a saucepan; bring to boiling. Combine sour cream or yogurt and cornstarch. Stir into juices. Cook and stir over medium heat till thickened and bubbly. Cook and stir 2 minutes more. Slice meat and serve with gravy. Makes 6 servings.

Per serving: 262 calories, 15 g total fat (6 g saturated), 73 mg cholesterol, 365 mg sodium, 4 g carbohydrate, 0 g fiber, 26 g protein.
Daily Values: 5% vitamin A, 1% vitamin C, 4% calcium, 9% iron.

For more flavor of Germany, heat a can of Bavarian-style sauerkraut in a saucepan. And for a quick, colorful complement, cook fresh green beans in the microwave oven. Add a basketful of rye rolls to the table, too.

Prep: 25 minutes
Cook: 4 to 10 hours

GOLDEN-GLAZED PORK RIBS

You'll love the honey-mustard glaze on these meaty ribs, but if you're concerned about sodium in your diet use low-sodium soy sauce; this saves you about 360 mg sodium per serving.

For a picnic-style supper, include coleslaw from the deli and corn muffins from the bakery on your menu.

Prep: 10 minutes
Bake: 1½ to 1¾ hours

2½ to 3 pounds pork loin back ribs or
     spareribs
¼ cup soy sauce

2 tablespoons Dijon-style mustard
2 tablespoons honey

1 Cut ribs into serving-size pieces. Place ribs, boneside down, on a rack in a shallow roasting pan.

2 Bake in a 350° oven for 1 hour. Drain off any fat.

3 For glaze, stir together the soy sauce, mustard, and honey. Brush ribs lightly with some of the glaze. Bake for 30 to 45 minutes more or till ribs are tender, brushing occasionally with glaze. Makes 4 to 6 servings.

Per serving: 539 calories, 38 g total fat (14 g saturated), 149 mg cholesterol, 1,333 mg sodium, 11 g carbohydrate, 0 g fiber, 37 g protein.
Daily Values: 0% vitamin A, 0% vitamin C, 5% calcium, 18% iron.

ROAST PORK WITH CORN-CHILI SAUCE

While the roast is in the oven, bake a casserole of candied sweet potatoes: In a 1½-quart casserole add a drained 16-ounce can sweet potatoes; top with 2 tablespoons brown sugar and 1 tablespoon margarine or butter. Add another drained 16-ounce can of sweet potatoes and top with 2 tablespoons brown sugar and 1 table-spoon margarine or butter. Bake, uncovered, in the 325° oven for 45 to 50 minutes or till potatoes are heated through and lightly glazed, spooning liquid over potatoes once or twice.

Prep: 15 minutes
Bake: 1¼ hours

1 2- to 2½-pound boneless pork top loin roast (single loin)
¼ teaspoon garlic salt
⅛ teaspoon pepper
¼ cup chopped onion
½ cup water

1 8-ounce can cream-style corn
½ medium red sweet pepper, cut into bite-size strips
1 to 2 tablespoons canned chopped green chili peppers

1 Place pork roast on a rack in a shallow roasting pan. Sprinkle with garlic salt and pepper.

2 Roast pork in a 325° oven for 1¼ hours or till center is barely pink and juices run clear (thermometer inserted near the center of the roast should register 160°). Remove meat to a platter; keep warm.

3 Meanwhile, for sauce, in a small saucepan cook onion uncovered in the water, gently boiling for 2 minutes. Stir in undrained corn, red pepper, and chili peppers. Return to boiling; simmer, uncovered, for 2 to 3 minutes or till sweet pepper is crisp-tender.

4 Slice meat; serve with sauce. Makes 6 servings.

Per serving: 301 calories, 19 g total fat (7 g saturated), 80 mg cholesterol, 250 mg sodium, 8 g carbohydrate, 1 g fiber, 23 g protein.
Daily Values: 5% vitamin A, 27% vitamin C, 0% calcium, 7% iron.

PORK CHOPS WITH APPLE RICE PILAF

For a faster dinner, skip browning the chops; instead, sprinkle the raw chops with the lemon-pepper seasoning plus paprika to add more color.

Complement the pork and rice pilaf with a slice of acorn squash drizzled with butter and maple syrup, and bake, covered, alongside the main dish till fork tender.

Prep: 20 minutes
Bake: 45 to 50 minutes

6 pork loin chops, rib chops, or shoulder chops, cut ¾ inch thick (about 1¾ pounds)
1 tablespoon cooking oil or olive oil
   Lemon-pepper seasoning
1 6-ounce package long grain and wild rice mix
1 20-ounce can sliced apples
2 tablespoons vinegar
1 cup water

1 Trim any separable fat from chops. In a 12-inch skillet brown chops on both sides in hot oil over medium-high heat. Sprinkle chops lightly with lemon-pepper seasoning.

2 In a 3-quart rectangular baking dish stir together the rice mix and seasoning packet. Combine undrained apples, vinegar, and water; pour evenly over rice. Top with chops. Cover dish tightly with foil.

3 Bake in a 350° oven for 45 to 50 minutes or till rice and chops are tender. Makes 6 servings.

Per serving: 341 calories, 11 g total fat (3 g saturated), 60 mg cholesterol, 573 mg sodium, 38 g carbohydrate, 0 g fiber, 22 g protein.
Daily Values: 0% vitamin A, 3% vitamin C, 0% calcium, 12% iron.

SAUSAGE AND CABBAGE SKILLET

1 small head cabbage, shredded
    (5 cups), or 5 cups preshredded
    cabbage with carrot
4 medium potatoes, sliced
1 medium onion, sliced and separated
    into rings
1 teaspoon caraway seed (optional)
1 pound fully cooked kielbasa or
    other smoked sausage link,
    halved lengthwise and bias-sliced
    into 1-inch pieces

1 cup apple juice
2 tablespoons brown or prepared
    mustard
½ teaspoon instant beef bouillon
    granules

Fully cooked sausage links are an easy answer to dinner because they need only to be heated through. However, longer simmering, as is done in this recipe, sometimes is preferred to develop the flavor of a dish.

Prep: 20 minutes
Cook: 30 minutes

1 In a 12-inch skillet combine cabbage, sliced potatoes, onion, and, if desired, caraway seed. Top with sausage.

2 In a small bowl combine apple juice, mustard, and bouillon granules. Pour over sausage mixture in skillet. Bring mixture to boiling; reduce heat. Cover and simmer about 30 minutes or till vegetables are tender. Serves 5.

Per serving: 483 calories, 28 g total fat (10 g saturated), 75 mg cholesterol, 1,041 mg sodium, 43 g carbohydrate, 4 g fiber, 15 g protein.
Daily Values: 0% vitamin A, 70% vitamin C, 7% calcium, 21% iron.

SAUSAGE SAVVY

You'll find many sausage varieties available today, such as Cajun and mesquite-flavored, that will add a new taste to your favorite recipes. Also, if you're concerned about fat in your diet, look for the lower-fat varieties of smoked sausage. They cut down on the fat, but not on the flavor.

CURRIED PORK AND PEA SOUP

1½ pounds boneless pork shoulder
     roast
1 cup yellow or green split peas
½ cup chopped carrot
½ cup chopped celery
½ cup chopped onion
1 49½-ounce can chicken broth
     (about 6 cups)

2 teaspoons curry powder
½ teaspoon paprika
¼ teaspoon ground cumin
¼ teaspoon pepper
2 cups frozen peas

When you come in from the cold on a blustery winter day, one sniff of this soup will warm you through and through. Take off your coat and boots, then preheat your oven to bake brown-and-serve rolls. When the rolls are ready, stir the frozen peas into the soup, and serve. Any lingering thoughts about the cold and snow will soon melt away.

1 Trim fat from pork. Cut pork into ½-inch pieces. Rinse and drain the split peas.

2 In a 3½- to 4-quart crockery cooker combine the split peas, carrot, celery, and onion. Add the broth, curry powder, paprika, cumin, and pepper. Stir in pork.

3 Cover and cook on low-heat setting for 10 to 12 hours or on high-heat setting for 4 hours. Stir in frozen peas; heat through, then serve. Makes 6 to 8 servings.

 Prep: 20 minutes
Cook: 4 to 12 hours

Per serving: 384 calories, 14 g total fat (4 g saturated), 75 mg cholesterol, 855 mg sodium, 30 g carbohydrate, 4 g fiber, 35 g protein.
Daily Values: 38% vitamin A, 12% vitamin C, 4% calcium, 28% iron.

HAM AND LENTIL SOUP

Love homemade bread, but not the work? Blender popovers are the easy answer. In a blender container combine 2 eggs, 1 cup milk, 1 tablespoon cooking oil, 1 cup all-purpose flour, and ¼ teaspoon salt. Blend till smooth. Pour batter into six greased 6-ounce custard cups. Bake in a 400° oven about 40 minutes or till firm. Prick with a fork before serving.

Prep: 10 minutes
Cook: 3¾ to 8¼ hours

1 cup dry lentils	1 teaspoon bottled minced garlic or 2 cloves garlic, minced
4 cups water	½ teaspoon grated lemon peel
1 medium onion, chopped	¼ teaspoon ground red pepper
1 cup chopped celery	1 cup cubed fully cooked ham
1 cup sliced carrot	2 cups chopped fresh spinach
2 teaspoons instant chicken bouillon granules	

1 Rinse and drain lentils.

2 In a crockery cooker combine lentils, water, onion, celery, carrot, bouillon granules, garlic, lemon peel, and red pepper.

3 Cover and cook on low-heat setting for 7 to 8 hours or on high-heat setting for 3½ to 4 hours. Add ham. Cook, covered, on high-heat setting for 10 minutes more. Stir in spinach; serve immediately. Makes 4 to 6 servings.

Per serving: 273 calories, 4 g total fat (1 g saturated), 21 mg cholesterol, 1,034 mg sodium, 38 g carbohydrate, 10 g fiber, 23 g protein.
Daily Values: 121% vitamin A, 41% vitamin C, 11% calcium, 44% iron.

BEEF AND BARLEY SOUP

1 pound boneless beef chuck pot
    roast, cut into ¼- to ½-inch cubes
7 cups water
1 cup chopped onion
2 stalks celery, chopped
2 tablespoons instant beef bouillon
    granules
½ teaspoon dried thyme, crushed

½ teaspoon dried marjoram, crushed
½ teaspoon dried basil, crushed
¼ teaspoon pepper
½ cup pearl barley or 1 cup quick-
    cooking pearl barley
1 10-ounce package frozen mixed
    vegetables

1 In a Dutch oven combine beef, water, onion, celery, bouillon granules, thyme, marjoram, basil, and pepper. Bring to boiling. Stir in pearl barley (if using); return to boiling. Reduce heat; cover and simmer for 45 minutes. (If using quick-cooking pearl barley, add the last 20 minutes of cooking.)

2 Stir frozen vegetables into soup*. Cook, covered, for 10 minutes more or till meat, barley, and vegetables are tender. Makes 6 servings.

*Note: If you want to add even more color, flavor, and nutrition to this delicious good-for-you soup, stir in ½ of a 10-ounce package frozen chopped spinach with the other frozen vegetables.

Per serving: 281 calories, 8 g total fat (3 g saturated), 76 mg cholesterol, 969 mg sodium, 22 g carbohydrate, 3 g fiber, 30 g protein.
Daily Values: 20% vitamin A, 8% vitamin C, 4% calcium, 28% iron.

Keep refrigerated bread-sticks on hand so you can bake these easy lemon-pepper breadsticks any-time: Stir together ½ tea-spoon finely shredded lemon peel, 1 tablespoon water, 1 tablespoon lemon juice, ¼ teaspoon salt, and ¼ to ½ teaspoon coarsely ground pepper. Using one package (8) refrigerated breadsticks, arrange the dough on a baking sheet, twisting ends of each breadstick several times in opposite directions. Brush twists with the lemon mix-ture and bake according to package directions. Serve warm with soup.

Prep: 25 minutes
Cook: 55 minutes

SPLIT PEA AND LENTIL SOUP

If you prefer, use your crockery cooker to simmer this soup. Combine all ingredients except the yogurt and use 4 cups of broth instead of 5. Cover and cook on low-heat setting for 7 to 8 hours or on high-heat setting for 3½ to 4 hours. Serve as directed.

Prep: 15 minutes
Cook: 1 hour

½ cup split peas
½ cup lentils
5 cups chicken broth or vegetable broth
¾ cup sliced carrot
¾ cup sliced celery
1 medium red sweet pepper, chopped, or ¼ cup chopped roasted red sweet pepper
1 medium onion, chopped
1 bay leaf
1 teaspoon ground cumin
¼ teaspoon pepper
¼ cup plain yogurt

1 Rinse and drain split peas and lentils. In a Dutch oven combine peas, lentils, broth, carrot, celery, sweet pepper, onion, bay leaf, cumin, and pepper.

2 Bring mixture to boiling. Reduce heat and simmer, covered, for 1 hour or till peas and lentils are tender. (Or, cover and bake in a 350° oven about 2 hours or till the lentils and split peas are tender.)

3 Remove bay leaf. Top each serving with yogurt. Makes 4 servings.

Per serving: 231 calories, 1 g total fat (0 g saturated), 0 mg cholesterol, 562 mg sodium, 41 g carbohydrate, 7 g fiber, 16 g protein.
Daily Values: 76% vitamin A, 125% vitamin C, 8% calcium, 32% iron.

SHREDDED BEEF WITH PICKLED PEPPERS

1 2½- to 3-pound boneless beef chuck pot roast, cut into 1-inch cubes
1 cup chopped onion
¼ cup Worcestershire sauce
1 tablespoon instant beef bouillon granules
1 teaspoon dried oregano, crushed
½ teaspoon dried basil, crushed

½ teaspoon dried thyme, crushed
1 teaspoon bottled minced garlic or 2 cloves garlic, minced
½ cup chopped canned pepperoncini (Italian pickled peppers) or other pickled peppers
8 hoagie buns, rye buns, or Kaiser rolls, split and toasted
6 ounces sliced Swiss cheese

1 In a 3½- to 4-quart crockery cooker combine the meat, onion, Worcestershire sauce, bouillon granules, oregano, basil, thyme, and garlic. Stir to mix.

2 Cover and cook on low-heat setting about 10 hours or on high-heat setting for 5 to 6 hours. Stir to break up meat cubes. Stir in chopped peppers.

3 Cook, uncovered, on high-heat setting for 30 minutes more, stirring often to break up meat.

4 Using a slotted spoon, place meat mixture on bottoms of toasted buns. Top with cheese. Broil 4 inches from heat about 1 minute or till cheese melts. Add tops of buns. Makes 8 servings.

Per serving: 493 calories, 18 g total fat (8 g saturated), 122 mg cholesterol, 1,009 mg sodium, 35 g carbohydrate, 2 g fiber, 46 g protein.
Daily Values: 42% vitamin A, 11% vitamin C, 20% calcium, 36% iron.

About 15 to 20 minutes before you're ready to serve dinner, turn on the oven to bake a batch of frozen potatoes. When the potatoes are done, remove them and turn on the broiler. Toast the cut sides of buns under the broiler, then assemble the sandwiches except for the bun tops. Return meat-topped buns to broiler to melt cheese.

Save those delicious meat juices! Serve them with the sandwiches for dipping—they'll make the sandwiches moister and add even more great flavor.

Prep: 25 minutes
Cook: 5½ to 10½ hours

BARBECUE BEEF SANDWICHES

For a quick side salad, cook a 16-ounce bag of loose-pack frozen vegetables such as broccoli and cauliflower; drain and quick-chill in the freezer for 15 minutes. At serving time, toss with Italian salad dressing and chopped tomato (seed the tomato first, if desired).

Prep: 30 minutes
Cook: 10 hours

1 2½- to 3-pound fresh beef brisket
1 10-ounce can tomatoes with green chili peppers
1 8-ounce can applesauce
½ of a 6-ounce can tomato paste (⅓ cup)

¼ cup soy sauce
¼ cup packed brown sugar
1 tablespoon Worcestershire sauce
10 to 12 hamburger buns, toasted

1 Trim excess fat from beef. Place meat in a 3½- to 6-quart crockery cooker. (If necessary, cut meat to fit.)

2 Stir together the undrained tomatoes with chili peppers, applesauce, tomato paste, soy sauce, brown sugar, and Worcestershire sauce; pour over meat.

3 Cover and cook on low-heat setting* about 10 hours or till meat is tender. Remove meat from juices; keep warm. Pour juices into a large saucepan. Bring to boiling; reduce heat. Boil gently, uncovered, for 15 to 20 minutes or till reduced to desired consistency, stirring frequently.

4 Thinly slice meat across the grain. For each sandwich, place several thin slices of meat on toasted bun; top with sauce. Makes 10 servings.

*Note: Beef brisket needs long, slow cooking to become tender, so using the high-heat setting on a crockery cooker is not recommended for this recipe.

Per serving: 309 calories, 12 g total fat (4 g saturated), 78 mg cholesterol, 661 mg sodium, 23 g carbohydrate, 1 g fiber, 27 g protein.
Daily Values: 3% vitamin A, 14% vitamin C, 3% calcium, 24% iron.

FIVE-SPICE PORK SANDWICHES AU JUS

1 2½- to 3-pound pork shoulder roast
1 cup apple juice
2 tablespoons soy sauce
2 tablespoons hoisin sauce

1½ teaspoons five-spice powder
6 to 8 kaiser rolls, split and toasted
1½ to 2 cups shredded Chinese
    cabbage

1 Trim any excess fat from roast. If necessary, cut roast to fit into a 3½- or 4-quart crockery cooker. Place meat in cooker.

2 For sauce, in a small bowl combine apple juice, soy sauce, hoisin sauce, and five-spice powder. Pour over roast.

3 Cover; cook on low-heat setting for 10 to 12 hours or on high-heat setting for 5 to 6 hours.

4 Remove roast from cooker. Remove meat from bone; discard bone and fat. Using two forks, shred meat. Skim fat from cooking juices. Divide juices among 6 to 8 bowls. Serve meat on toasted rolls with shredded cabbage. Serve with juices. Makes 6 to 8 servings.

Per serving: 444 calories, 18 g total fat (6 g saturated), 101 mg cholesterol, 37 g carbohydrate, 2 g fiber, 851 mg sodium, 33 g protein.
Daily Values: 3% vitamin A, 10% vitamin C, 8% calcium, 24% iron.

Look for five-spice powder in the Oriental section of your supermarket or make your own: In a blender container combine 3 tablespoons ground cinnamon; 6 star anise or 2 teaspoons aniseed, 1½ teaspoons fennel seed, 1½ teaspoons whole szechwan peppers or whole black peppers, and ¾ teaspoon ground cloves. Cover; blend to a fine powder. Store in a tightly covered container. Makes ⅓ cup.

Current nutrition guidelines suggest 5-a-day—that is, 5 full servings of fruits and vegetables each day. It's easy to meet that goal when you serve crunchy vegetables with fast-fixin' sandwiches like this one.

Prep: 30 minutes
Cook: 5 to 12 hours

JUMP- START RECIPES

Begin with Master Mixes

In the kitchen—as in life—starting with a good base greatly improves your chances of success. And the recipes in this chapter are confirmation indeed. Four super-star starters— Italian Sauce, Mexican Meat Mix, Browned Mushroom Sauce, and Marvelous Meatballs— form the core for 14 fantastic dinners. Simply thaw the mix of your choice, then make the meal of your choice. From Mexican Pita Pizza to Sweet and Sour Meatball Stew, these recipes will prove you're worthy of the title master chef.

BASIC ITALIAN SAUCE

Prep: 25 minutes   **Cook:** 50 minutes

In a large saucepan or Dutch oven cook 2 cups chopped *onion,* 1 cup chopped *green sweet pepper,* ½ cup chopped *celery,* and 2 teaspoons *bottled minced garlic or 4 cloves garlic* (chopped) in 2 tablespoons hot *cooking oil* till tender but not brown. Stir in four 16-ounce cans *diced tomatoes* (undrained), two 6-ounce cans *tomato paste,* ⅔ cup *water,* ¼ cup snipped fresh *parsley,* 2 teaspoons *sugar,* 2 teaspoons dried *basil* (crushed), 2 teaspoons dried *oregano* (crushed), 2 teaspoons dried *marjoram* (crushed), 1 teaspoon *salt,* and ½ teaspoon *pepper.* Bring to boiling; reduce heat. Cover and simmer for 30 minutes. Uncover and simmer 10 to 15 minutes more or to desired consistency. Cool. Divide into four 2½-cup portions in freezer containers; seal, label, and freeze. Use as needed, thawing first. Makes about 10 cups.

Note: You can use one portion of this mix immediately without freezing to prepare any of the recipes on pages 146–151. Also, you can substitute one 27- to 30-ounce jar meatless spaghetti sauce in place of the Basic Italian Sauce in any of those recipes.

ZITI WITH CREAMY SAUSAGE MARINARA

To thaw one frozen 2½-cup portion of Basic Italian Sauce, transfer to a microwave-safe bowl and heat on 70% power (medium-high) for 12 to 14 minutes, stirring occasionally, or thaw overnight in the refrigerator.

Pasta has become part of the All-American meals. And, Americans love a tossed salad with their pasta. For a change of pace, serve the salad after the pasta, as the French often do.

Prep: 10 minutes
Cook: 25 minutes

  8 **ounces pasta such as ziti, tagliati, rigatoni, or mostaccioli**
12 **ounces fresh Italian sausage links, sliced**
  1 **2½-cup portion Basic Italian Sauce, thawed (see recipe, above)**

⅓ **cup whipping cream, half-and-half, or light cream**
    Shredded Parmesan cheese (optional)

1 Cook pasta according to package directions. Drain; keep warm. Meanwhile, in a 2-quart saucepan cook sliced sausage over medium heat till cooked through, turning frequently. Drain well.

2 Add thawed Basic Italian sauce to saucepan with sausage; bring to boiling. Stir in cream; heat through. Toss with hot pasta; sprinkle with Parmesan cheese, if desired. Makes 4 servings.

Per serving: 623 calories, 28 g total fat (10 g saturated), 76 mg cholesterol, 1,293 mg sodium, 69 g carbohydrate, 0 g fiber, 24 g protein.
Daily Values: 42% vitamin A, 69% vitamin C, 8% calcium, 32% iron.

ITALIAN SEAFOOD FETTUCCINE

You can use fresh shrimp in the shell for this recipe, if you like. Start with about 10 ounces. Peel and devein the shrimp, then rinse well. Add to boiling sauce and cook, uncovered, 3 to 5 minutes or till shrimp are pink, then add the ham. If the shrimp are very large, cut them in half lengthwise before adding to the sauce. Crispy breadsticks—with or without sesame seeds or poppy seeds—round out this Italiano meal.

Prep: 10 minutes
Cook: 25 minutes

8 ounces fettuccine or linguine
  Nonstick spray coating
	6 ounces cooked peeled and
	  deveined shrimp

1½ cups sliced fresh mushrooms	½ cup chopped ham

1 2½-cup portion Basic Italian Sauce,
  thawed (see recipe, page 146)
	Freshly grated Romano cheese
	  (optional)

1 Cook pasta according to package directions. Drain; keep warm. Meanwhile, spray a 2- or 3-quart saucepan with nonstick coating. Cook mushrooms about 5 minutes or till tender.

2 Add thawed Basic Italian Sauce to mushrooms; bring to boiling. Stir in cooked shrimp and ham; heat through. Serve over hot cooked pasta. Sprinkle with freshly grated Romano cheese, if desired. Makes 4 servings.

Per serving: 499 calories, 6 g total fat (1 g saturated), 93 mg cholesterol, 1,040 mg sodium, 69 g carbohydrate, 1 g fiber, 25 g protein.
Daily Values: 36% vitamin A, 70% vitamin C, 8% calcium, 39% iron.

EASY LASAGNE

6 ounces lean ground beef, ground pork, or pork sausage	⅓ cup grated Parmesan cheese
1 2½-cup portion Basic Italian Sauce, thawed (see recipe, page 146)	1 tablespoon snipped fresh basil or 1 teaspoon dried basil, crushed
1½ cups ricotta cheese	¼ teaspoon pepper
1 cup chopped fresh spinach or ½ of a 10-ounce package frozen chopped spinach, thawed and drained	¼ teaspoon ground nutmeg
	9 lasagne noodles
	1¼ cups hot water (140°)
	1 cup shredded mozzarella or provolone cheese (4 ounces)

1 In a medium saucepan cook ground meat till brown. Drain off any fat. Add thawed Basic Italian Sauce. In a medium bowl stir together the ricotta cheese, spinach, Parmesan, basil, pepper, and nutmeg.

2 Lightly grease a 2-quart rectangular baking dish. Place 3 of the uncooked noodles on the bottom of the dish. Spoon one-third of the meat sauce over the noodles. Top with half of the spinach mixture and 3 more uncooked noodles. Spoon another third of the meat sauce over the second layer of noodles; top with remaining spinach mixture. Place the last 3 noodles on and spoon remaining meat on top.*

3 Slowly pour hot water into dish around the edges. Cover dish tightly with foil and bake in a 375° oven for 40 minutes. Uncover and sprinkle with mozzarella or provolone cheese. Bake, uncovered, about 15 minutes or till noodles are tender and casserole is bubbly around the edges. Let stand for 10 minutes. Cut into squares to serve. Makes 6 to 8 servings.

*Note: If desired, cover the unbaked lasagne with plastic wrap and chill for up to 24 hours. Before baking, uncover the dish and add the hot water, increasing it to 1⅓ cups.

Per serving: 517 calories, 17 g total fat (8 g saturated), 51 mg cholesterol, 509 mg sodium, 62 g carbohydrate, 2 g fiber, 29 g protein.
Daily Values: 27% vitamin A, 42% vitamin C, 35% calcium, 31% iron.

Round out the basil-spiked lasagne with cooked baby carrots.

When your summer herb garden wanes, dried herbs can pinch hit for the fresh variety. Use the following substitution levels, tasting your dish after adding a dried herb, and increasing the amount as desired.

Strong-flavored herbs such as thyme, marjoram, sage, rosemary, tarragon, and dillweed: Use ½ teaspoon dried herb for each tablespoon fresh herb.

Mild-flavored herbs such as basil, oregano, mint, and savory: Use about 1 teaspoon dried herb for each tablespoon fresh herb.

Prep: 25 minutes
Cook: 55 minutes

MEXICAN MEAT MIX

Prep: 10 minutes **Cook:** 10 minutes

In a 12-inch skillet cook 2 pounds *lean ground beef, pork, or lamb* till meat is brown; drain off any fat. Drain well on paper towels; return meat to skillet. Stir in 4 cups *red chunky salsa* and one 15-ounce can and one 8-ounce can *red kidney beans* (drained). Divide into four 2-cup portions in freezer containers; seal, label, and freeze. Use as needed, thawing first. Makes about 8 cups.

Note: You can use one portion of this mix immediately without freezing to prepare any of the recipes on pages 153–159.

TACO SALAD

1 2-cup portion Mexican Meat Mix, thawed (see recipe, above)
½ cup salsa
4 cups shredded lettuce
2 cups chopped tomatoes
1 large green or red sweet pepper, cut into strips
½ cup sliced green onion

2 cups shredded cheddar or Monterey Jack cheese (8 ounces)
Tortilla chips
Frozen avocado dip, thawed (optional)
Dairy sour cream (optional)
Pickled jalapeño peppers or pepperoncini peppers (optional)

1 In a 1½-quart saucepan heat thawed Mexican Meat Mix. Stir in salsa; heat through.

2 Place lettuce on four plates. Top with tomatoes, sweet peppers, and green onion. Spoon hot meat mixture over salad; sprinkle with cheese. Serve with tortilla chips. Dollop with avocado dip and sour cream, if desired. Garnish with peppers, if desired. Makes 4 servings.

Per serving: 597 calories, 39 g total fat (18 g saturated), 101 mg cholesterol, 1,126 mg sodium, 36 g carbohydrate, 7 g fiber, 33 g protein.
Daily Values: 60% vitamin A, 203% vitamin C, 42% calcium, 29% iron.

To thaw one frozen 2-cup portion of Mexican Meat Mix in your microwave oven, transfer to a microwave-safe bowl and heat on 70% power (medium-high) for 12 minutes, stirring occasionally. To thaw in the refrigerator, remove one portion from the freezer and let it stand overnight in the refrigerator.

Cook: 10 minutes
Prep: 20 minutes

CHILI PIE

No need for pastry cloth or floury surface when you make this recipe—the crust is done right in the pie plate. The result: No countertop catastrophes, which saves you the time of having to clean it up. Use this crust recipe for your other favorite main-dish pies, too. Chili Pie needs just a touch of cool, crispness on the side. Try coleslaw, vegetable crudités, or your best-loved tossed salad.

Prep: 15 minutes
Cook: 25 minutes

1⅓ cups all-purpose flour
⅓ cup cornmeal
1 teaspoon sugar
¼ teaspoon salt
⅓ cup cooking oil
⅓ cup milk
1 2-cup portion Mexican Meat Mix, thawed (see recipe, page 153)

1 8-ounce can whole-kernel corn, drained
½ medium green sweet pepper, cut into thin rings
½ cup shredded cheddar or Monterey Jack cheese (2 ounces)
Dairy sour cream

1 For crust, in a 9-inch pie plate stir together flour, cornmeal, sugar, and salt; mix well. In a 1-cup glass measure stir together the oil and milk. Pour all at once over the flour mixture. MIx with a fork till flour is completely moistened. With your fingers, pat the dough evenly on sides and bottom of pie plate.

2 Bake in a 425° oven for 10 minutes. Remove from oven.

3 Meanwhile, in a 1½-quart saucepan combine the thawed Mexican Meat Mix and the corn; heat, covered, over medium heat. Spoon meat mixture into pie crust. Top with sweet pepper rings and cheese. Return pie to oven and bake about 15 minutes more or till heated through. Dollop servings with sour cream. Makes 4 to 6 servings.

Per serving: 646 calories, 36 g total fat (10 g saturated), 57 mg cholesterol, 849 mg sodium, 63 g carbohydrate, 5 g fiber, 26 g protein.
Daily Values: 22% vitamin A, 72% vitamin C, 15% calcium, 35% iron.

SOFT SHELL TACO PIE

Trim even more time when preparing this recipe by using preshredded cheese. You'll find packages of your favorite cheeses—including cheddar, Monterey Jack, mozzarella, and various blends—already shredded in your grocery store's dairy section. Remember, too: Shredded cheese weighs in at 4 ounces equalling 1 cup.

Prep: 20 minutes
Cook: 25 to 30 minutes

1 tablespoon all-purpose flour
1 8-ounce carton dairy sour cream
¾ cup shredded cheddar or Monterey Jack cheese (3 ounces)
¼ cup canned diced green chili peppers, drained
2 tablespoons milk
Nonstick spray coating or 1 teaspoon cooking oil

3 10-inch flour tortillas
1 2-cup portion Mexican Meat Mix, thawed (see recipe, page 153)
1 cup shredded lettuce
1 small tomato, cut into wedges
1 ripe avocado, cut into wedges (optional)

1 In a bowl stir flour into sour cream. Add ½ cup of the shredded cheese, the chili peppers, and milk; mix well. Spray a 9-inch pie plate with nonstick coating. Place one tortilla in the plate.

2 Top with about ⅔ cup of the thawed Mexican Meat Mix and one-third of the sour cream mixture. Repeat with another tortilla, another ⅔ cup Mexican Meat Mix, and another third of the sour cream mixture. Cover with remaining tortilla, remaining Mexican Meat Mix, and remaining sour cream mixture.

3 Bake, uncovered, in a 350° oven for 25 to 30 minutes or till heated through. Sprinkle remaining ¼ cup cheese over pie. Let stand 5 minutes before cutting into wedges to serve. Serve with shredded lettuce, tomato wedges, and, if desired, avocado wedges. Makes 4 servings.

Per serving: 471 calories, 30 g total fat (1 g saturated), 83 mg cholesterol, 651 mg sodium, 31 g carbohydrate, 3 g fiber, 24 g protein.
Daily Values: 29% vitamin A, 44% vitamin C, 25% calcium, 21% iron.

MEXICAN PITA PIZZA

3 large whole wheat pita bread
  rounds, split horizontally
1 cup shredded cheddar cheese
  (4 ounces)
1 2-cup portion Mexican Meat Mix,
  thawed (see recipe, page 153)
1 4-ounce can diced green chili
  peppers, drained

Shredded cheddar cheese
Shredded lettuce
Chopped tomato
Dairy sour cream (optional)
Snipped cilantro (optional)

Pita bread is a round, flat Middle Eastern unleavened bread usually cut in half vertically to form pockets for sandwiches. In this recipe, cutting them horizontally creates perfect individual pizzas.

Tame the tingle of the chili peppers and the meat sauce by accompanying this dish with fresh fruit.

1 Place pitas on a large ungreased baking sheet; do not overlap. Divide the 1 cup cheese equally among the pitas. Spoon meat mixture over cheese. Sprinkle with chili peppers.

2 Bake, uncovered, in a 425° oven for 10 to 15 minutes or till hot and cheese is melted. To serve, top with additional cheese, lettuce, tomato, and, if desired, sour cream and cilantro. Makes 6 servings.

Prep: 15 minutes
Cook: 10 to 15 minutes

Per serving: 284 calories, 17 g total fat (7 g saturated), 48 mg cholesterol, 647 mg sodium, 20 g carbohydrate, 2 g fiber, 18 g protein.
Daily Values: 17% vitamin A, 48% vitamin C, 17% calcium, 15% iron.

BROWNED MUSHROOM SAUCE

Prep: 15 minutes **Cook:** 18 minutes

In a 4½-quart Dutch oven combine ⅓ cup *cooking oil,* ¼ cup *all-purpose flour,* and 3 tablespoons *margarine or butter.* Cook and stir over medium heat till golden brown. Stir in 6 cups sliced fresh *mushrooms,* ¾ cup finely chopped *onion,* ¾ teaspoon dried *thyme* (crushed), ½ teaspoon *salt,* and ½ teaspoon *pepper.* Cook and stir till onion is tender. Combine 3 cups *beef broth* and ⅓ cup *cornstarch;* add to mushroom mixture along with 3 cups *milk, half-and-half, or light cream.* Cook and stir till thickened and bubbly; cook 2 minutes more. Divide into three 2⅔-cup portions in freezer containers; seal, label, and freeze. Use as needed, thawing first. Makes about 8 cups sauce.

Note: You can use one portion of this mix immediately without freezing to prepare any of the recipes on pages 160–164.

TURKEY-MUSHROOM BAKED POTATOES

You can thaw frozen Browned Mushroom Sauce in any of four ways:

1. Transfer a portion to a microwave-safe bowl. Micro-cook, uncovered, on 30% power (medium-low) 8 to 12 minutes; stir once.

2. Place one freezer container of sauce in warm water for 1 hour.

3. Transfer one portion of frozen sauce to a heavy saucepan; heat, covered, over medium-low heat 15 minutes or till thawed, stirring occasionally.

4. Let one portion thaw overnight in the refrigerator.

Prep: 10 minutes
Bake: 40 to 60 minutes

4　medium baking potatoes
　　Cooking oil (optional)
1　2⅔-cup portion Browned
　　Mushroom Sauce, thawed (see
　　recipe, above)
2　ounces process Gruyère or process
　　Swiss cheese, cut up

2　cups chopped cooked turkey or
　　chicken (10 ounces)
1　small red sweet pepper, cut into
　　strips (optional)
1　tablespoon snipped fresh parsley
　　(optional)

1 Scrub potatoes; pat dry. Prick with a fork. If desired, rub with small amount cooking oil. Bake in 425° oven for 40 to 60 minutes or till tender. (Or, cook the 4 potatoes in the microwave on 100% power [high] for 13 to 16 minutes, rearranging once.)

2 In a 3-quart saucepan heat thawed Browned Mushroom Sauce to boiling. Add cheese; stir till cheese is melted. Add turkey or chicken; heat through. Cut potatoes open and serve turkey mixture over potatoes. Top with sweet pepper strips and sprinkle with parsley, if desired. Makes 4 servings.

Per serving: 536 calories, 22 g total fat (7 g saturated), 78 mg cholesterol, 459 mg sodium, 52 g carbohydrate, 2 g fiber, 32 g protein.
Daily Values: 12% vitamin A, 47% vitamin C, 22% calcium, 29% iron.

CHICKEN AND MUSHROOM FETTUCCINE

8 ounces fettuccine or linguine
2 cups small broccoli flowerettes
1 2⅔-cup portion frozen Browned
   Mushroom Sauce, thawed (see
   recipe, page 160)

2 tablespoons dry sherry or beef
   broth
6 to 8 ounces cooked chicken or
   smoked chicken breast, cut into
   bite-size pieces
   Fresh thyme sprigs (optional)

1 Cook pasta according to package directions, adding the broccoli flowerettes during the last 4 minutes of cooking. Drain. Cover and keep warm.

2 Meanwhile, in a 2-quart saucepan heat thawed Browned Mushroom Sauce just to boiling. Add sherry or broth; whisk till sauce is smooth. Stir in chicken; heat through. Serve over hot pasta mixture. Garnish with thyme, if desired. Makes 4 servings.

Per serving: 495 calories, 15 g total fat (3 g saturated), 43 mg cholesterol, 411 mg sodium, 63 g carbohydrate, 5 g fiber, 27 g protein.
Daily Values: 25% vitamin A, 66% vitamin C, 12% calcium, 4% iron.

Fettuccine and linguine are available in both dried and refrigerated forms at the supermarket. Each needs a slightly different cooking time: The dried pastas take about 8 to 10 minutes, and the refrigerated versions take only 1½ to 2 minutes. Also, when substituting a refrigerated pasta for the dried pasta called for in a recipe, double the amount of dried pasta called for to get enough for each serving. (The amount of pasta listed in this book's recipes, like most recipes, is for the dried form.)

Prep: 10 minutes
Cook: 25 minutes

CHEESY VEGETARIAN LASAGNE

Here's an easy way to add more Italian flair to your fare. Cut one 16-ounce loaf Italian bread (about 14 inches long) in half horizontally. In a small bowl, stir together ⅔ cup mayonnaise or salad dressing, ½ cup grated Parmesan or Romano cheese, and 1 tablespoon purchased pesto. Spread over cut sides of bread. Place bread, pesto side up, on unheated rack of a broiler pan. Broil 4 to 5 inches from heat for 2 to 3 minutes or till bubbly. Sprinkle lightly with crushed red pepper. Cut diagonally into 2-inch slices. Makes 14 slices.

Prep: 35 minutes
Cook: 35 minutes

9 no-boil lasagne noodles or regular lasagne noodles
1 2⅔-cup portion Browned Mushroom Sauce, thawed (see recipe, page 160)
1 15- or 16-ounce can butter beans or great northern beans, drained
½ cup chopped red or green sweet pepper
1 beaten egg

2 cups shredded cheddar cheese (8 ounces)
1 cup shredded Monterey Jack cheese (4 ounces)
½ cup grated Parmesan cheese
½ cup ricotta cheese
2 tablespoons snipped fresh basil or 2 teaspoons dried basil, crushed
¼ teaspoon pepper

1 If using regular lasagne noodles, cook according to package directions. In a 3-quart saucepan heat thawed Browned Mushroom Sauce to boiling. Remove from heat. Stir in the beans and sweet pepper; set aside. In a medium bowl combine egg, 1 cup of the cheddar cheese, the Monterey Jack cheese, Parmesan cheese, and ricotta cheese. Stir in basil and pepper; set aside.

2 Lightly grease a 2-quart rectangular baking dish. Place 3 of the cooked regular noodles or 3 no-boil noodles on the bottom. Top with one-third of the mushroom sauce and half of the cheese mixture. Top with 3 more noodles, another third of the mushroom sauce, and remaining cheese mixture. Top with remaining 3 noodles and remaining mushroom sauce.

3 Bake, covered with foil, in a 375° oven for 30 minutes. Uncover and sprinkle with remaining 1 cup of cheddar cheese; return to oven. Bake, uncovered, for 5 minutes. Let stand 10 minutes; cut into squares to serve. Serves 6.

Per serving: 575 calories, 33 g total fat (18 g saturated), 115 mg cholesterol, 1,096 mg sodium, 36 g carbohydrate, 4 g fiber, 33 g protein.
Daily Values: 38% vitamin A, 24% vitamin C, 65% calcium, 20% iron.

MARVELOUS MEATBALLS

Prep: 20 minutes **Bake:** 25 minutes

In a large mixing bowl combine 2 beaten *eggs;* 1½ cups soft *bread crumbs* (2 slices); 1 cup finely chopped *onion;* ½ cup snipped fresh *parsley;* ½ cup *milk, beef broth, or chicken broth;* 1 teaspoon *salt;* ½ teaspoon dried *thyme* (crushed); and ½ teaspoon *pepper.* Add 2 pounds *lean ground beef, pork, lamb, chicken, or turkey;* mix well. Form into forty-eight 1¼- to 1½-inch balls. Place on a wire rack in a 15x10x2-inch baking pan or the unheated rack of a broiler pan. Bake in a 400° oven for 20 to 25 minutes or till no longer pink in center. Drain on paper towels. Divide into 2 portions of 24 meatballs each and place in freezer containers; seal, label, and freeze. Use as needed, thawing first. Makes 48 meatballs.

Note: You can use one portion of the meatballs immediately without freezing to prepare any of the recipes on pages 167–173.

CREAMY MEATBALLS AND MUSHROOMS OVER NOODLES

8 ounces egg noodles
1 2½-cup portion Browned Mushroom
   Sauce, thawed (see recipe,
   page 160)
1 24-meatball portion Marvelous
   Meatballs, thawed (see recipe,
   above)

½ teaspoon ground nutmeg or
   1 teaspoon dried dillweed,
   crushed
½ cup dairy sour cream
   Snipped fresh parsley

1 Cook noodles according to package directions. Cover and keep warm.

2 Meanwhile, in a large saucepan heat thawed Browned Mushroom Sauce till boiling. Add thawed Marvelous Meatballs and nutmeg or dillweed to sauce. Heat over medium heat till bubbly and meatballs are heated through. Add sour cream, stirring till well blended. Heat through over low heat; do not boil.

3 Serve meatball and mushroom mixture over hot cooked noodles. Sprinkle with parsley. Makes 4 to 6 servings.

Per serving: 695 calories, 36 g total fat (15 g saturated), 201 mg cholesterol, 769 mg sodium, 56 g carbohydrate, 1 g fiber, 35 g protein.
Daily Values: 18% vitamin A, 19% vitamin C, 16% calcium, 39% iron.

To thaw Marvelous Meatballs, let one portion stand overnight in the refrigerator. Or, spread them in a single layer in a 2-quart microwave-safe dish. Cover and cook on 100% power (high) for 4 to 6 minutes or till thawed, stirring once.

This meal cooks on your stove in a flash so let your microwave oven help you at the mealtime finish line. Just micro-cook a favorite vegetable and everything will be ready in 30 minutes.

Prep: 15 minutes
Cook: 15 minutes

SPAGHETTI AND MEATBALLS

Spaghetti and meatballs with a topping of Parmesan cheese—perfecto! Round out the meal with your favorite salad.

For a more poignant flavor, try fresh Parmesan cheese next time. You can grate or shred it with hand-held utensils or use a food processor. Or, you can cut it with a vegetable peeler into large pieces called shards for pasta with a powerful Parmesan punch. Your deli fresh out of the Parmesan? Then try fresh Romano cheese. It tastes similar to Parmesan, but has a slightly stronger flavor and aroma.

Prep: 20 minutes
Cook: 15 minutes

8 ounces spaghetti or fettuccine
3 cups sliced fresh mushrooms
1 tablespoon margarine or butter
1 2½-cup portion Basic Italian Sauce, thawed, (see recipe, page 146) or 2½ cups bottled meatless spaghetti sauce

1 24-meatball portion Marvelous Meatballs, thawed (see recipe, page 167)
Parmesan cheese

1 Cook pasta according to package directions; drain. Cover and keep warm.

2 Meanwhile, in a large saucepan cook mushrooms in hot margarine or butter till tender. Stir in Basic Italian Sauce or spaghetti sauce and Marvelous Meatballs; heat through.

3 Serve over hot cooked pasta. Top with Parmesan pieces or sprinkle with grated Parmesan. Makes 4 servings.

Per serving: 646 calories, 26 g total fat (8 g saturated), 127 mg cholesterol, 831 mg sodium, 69 g carbohydrate, 4 g fiber, 36 g protein.
Daily Values: 22% vitamin A, 71% vitamin C, 14% calcium, 49% iron.

ITALIAN MEATBALL SANDWICH

½ cup chopped green sweet pepper
1 medium onion, cut into wedges
2 tablespoons water
1 24-meatball portion Marvelous
   Meatballs, thawed (see recipe,
   page 167)

1 8-ounce can pizza sauce
4 Hoagie buns, French rolls, or
   Italian rolls
½ cup shredded provolone cheese
   (2 ounces)

1 In a large saucepan combine sweet pepper and onion; add water. Cover and cook over medium heat about 2 minutes or just till vegetables are crisp-tender; drain. Stir in thawed Marvelous Meatballs and pizza sauce. Heat through.

2 Cut top ½ inch from rolls. Open and scoop out some of the soft bread inside the bottom part. Spoon 6 meatballs inside each roll; spoon the sauce and vegetables over meatballs. Sprinkle with cheese. Top with tops of rolls. Place sandwiches, top sides up, in a 2-quart rectangular baking pan. Bake in a 400° oven for 10 to 15 minutes or till hot and crusty, and cheese is melted. Makes 4 servings.

Per serving: 759 calories, 26 g total fat (10 g saturated), 134 mg cholesterol, 1,613 mg sodium, 90 g carbohydrate, 5 g fiber, 40 g protein.
Daily Values: 22% vitamin A, 46% vitamin C, 19% calcium, 37% iron.

Be sure to save the scooped-out soft bread crumbs. You can use them in meat loaves or as casserole toppers, or even freeze them for adding to your next batch of Marvelous Meatballs.

Chips are a favorite for serving with sandwiches. Potato chips are tops, with tortilla chips rated high, too. For a change-of-chips, try pasta chips. These crunchy morsels are made by frying cooked pasta.

Prep: 15 minutes
Bake: 10 to 15 minutes

SWEET AND SOUR MEATBALL STEW

1 **20-ounce can pineapple chunks (juice pack)**

1 **medium green sweet pepper, cut into strips**

1 **medium red sweet pepper, cut into strips**

1 **cup beef broth**

2 **tablespoons red wine vinegar**

2 **tablespoons soy sauce**

1 **tablespoon dry sherry**

1 **teaspoon grated gingerroot or ½ teaspoon ground ginger**

½ **teaspoon bottled minced garlic or 1 clove garlic, minced**

1 **24-meatball portion Marvelous Meatballs, thawed (see recipe, page 167)**

2 **tablespoons cornstarch**

2 **tablespoons water**

2 **cups fresh pea pods or one 6-ounce package frozen pea pods**

3 **cups hot cooked rice**

1 In a 12-inch skillet combine undrained pineapple, sweet peppers, broth, vinegar, soy sauce, sherry, gingerroot or ginger, and garlic. Add Marvelous Meatballs. Bring to boiling; reduce heat.

2 Cover and simmer 10 to 15 minutes or till vegetables are crisp-tender and meatballs are heated through.

3 Combine cornstarch and water; stir into skillet. Cook and stir over medium heat till thickened and bubbly. Stir in pea pods; cook and stir 2 minutes more or till pea pods are heated through. Serve over hot cooked rice. Serves 4.

Per serving: 546 calories, 18 g total fat (7 g saturated), 124 mg cholesterol, 1,113 mg sodium, 66 g carbohydrate, 3 g fiber, 29 g protein.
Daily Values: 20% vitamin A, 79% vitamin C, 9% calcium, 37% iron.

When preparing rice for a meal, choose the long or short—cooking time, that is. Brown rice requires about 35 minutes to cook; white long grain rice is ready in a little less than 20 minutes. Quick-cooking brown and white rices need only about 10 minutes. If time allows, choose the slower-cooking brown rice—it adds more fiber to your meal, plus it has a nuttier taste.

Prep: 20 minutes
Cook: 12 to 17 minutes

MAKE-AHEAD DINNERS

You'll Love Coming Home to

Take advantage of free time—an evening or weekend afternoon, perhaps—to prepare meals ahead. (Consider enlisting the help of family members and turn your cookathon into a relaxing, fun family occasion.) Then, reap your reward on a harried day when a sensational meal is as near as the freezer or fridge. Imagine your family's delight when your answer to "What's for dinner?" is "Bean and Beef Enchilada Casserole" or "Mustard Crisp Chicken." All your smart planning and cooking ahead pays off deliciously.

MUSTARD CRISP CHICKEN

Since the chicken bakes in the oven, it makes sense to cook another part of your meal in it, too. Pair the crispy, zippy chicken with oven-baked new potatoes or baked squash, cooking them alongside the chicken on a second oven rack. Round out your no-hassle meal with a micro-cooked green vegetable such as asparagus, beans, or broccoli.

Prep: 15 minutes
Chill: 2 to 24 hours
Bake: 40 to 50 minutes

2½ pounds meaty chicken pieces, skin removed
½ cup Dijon-style mustard
1 tablespoon snipped fresh thyme or 1 teaspoon dried thyme, crushed
1 tablespoon water
½ teaspoon bottled minced garlic or 1 clove garlic, minced
¼ teaspoon pepper

¼ teaspoon paprika
⅛ teaspoon ground cinnamon
2 cups soft bread crumbs or 1¼ cups fine dry bread crumbs
2 tablespoons margarine or butter, melted

1 Rinse chicken; pat dry with paper towels. In a bowl combine mustard, thyme, water, garlic, pepper, paprika, and cinnamon. In another bowl or plastic bag place bread crumbs. Coat chicken with mustard mixture, then roll or shake in the bread crumbs. Arrange chicken in a 15x10x1-inch baking pan so pieces do not touch.

2 Cover pan with plastic wrap; refrigerate for 2 to 24 hours.

3 When ready to serve, drizzle chicken with melted margarine or butter. Bake chicken, uncovered, in a 375° oven for 40 to 50 minutes or till crisp and tender and no pink remains. Do not turn. Makes 6 servings.

Per serving: 245 calories, 11 g total fat (2 g saturated), 69 mg cholesterol, 688 mg sodium, 9 g carbohydrate, 0 g fiber, 25 g protein.
Daily Values: 6% vitamin A, 0% vitamin C, 3% calcium, 10% iron.

PIMIENTO CHICKEN

4 skinless, boneless chicken breast halves (about 1 pound)
1 tablespoon cooking oil
¾ cup chopped onion
1 teaspoon bottled minced garlic or 2 cloves garlic, minced
¾ cup parboiled (converted) rice
1 cup sliced fresh mushrooms

1 14½-ounce can chicken broth
½ cup dry white wine
⅛ teaspoon ground saffron
¼ teaspoon pepper
1½ cups frozen peas
1 2-ounce jar sliced pimiento, drained
Shredded Parmesan cheese

When freezing casseroles made with rice, be sure to use parboiled rice to prepare the recipe. This type of rice—also known as converted rice—stays firm when frozen; frozen cooked long grain white rice and brown rice tend to be mushy when reheated.

Prep: 35 minutes
Freeze: Up to 6 months
Bake: 1 to 1¼ hours

1 Rinse chicken; pat dry with paper towels. In a 10-inch skillet cook chicken in hot oil about 6 minutes or till no longer pink, turning once. Remove from skillet.

2 In the same skillet cook the onion and garlic in drippings till tender. Stir in uncooked rice and mushrooms. Add broth, wine, saffron, and pepper. Bring to boiling; reduce heat. Cover and simmer for 20 minutes or till tender*. Remove from heat. Stir in peas and pimiento. Cool.

3 Spoon rice mixture into 4 individual oven- or microwave-safe casseroles; place a piece of chicken in each, pressing it down into the rice. Cover with foil; seal, label, and freeze up to 6 months.

4 When ready to serve, bake frozen casseroles, covered, in a 350° oven for 1 to 1¼ hours. (Or, micro-cook 1 or 2 frozen casseroles, covered, on 70% power [medium-high] till hot, rearranging once. Allow 8 to 10 minutes for 1 dish, 13 to 16 minutes for 2 dishes.)

5 Sprinkle cheese over each serving. Makes 4 servings.

*Note: To assemble, then serve this dish immediately, return the chicken to the skillet the last 5 minutes while the rice cooks. Add the peas and pimiento; cover and cook 5 minutes more.

Per serving: 368 calories, 8 g total fat (2 g saturated), 48 mg cholesterol, 526 mg sodium, 42 g carbohydrate, 4 g fiber, 26 g protein.
Daily Values: 10% vitamin A, 33% vitamin C, 13% calcium, 24% iron.

PARMESAN CHICKEN AND BROCCOLI

Baby peeled carrots are the darling of the produce section. Just cook and eat. For a fast off-the-shelf dessert, simmer a 29-ounce can of sliced peaches (packed in light syrup) with 1 to 2 tablespoons margarine or butter and a cinnamon stick for about 5 minutes. Serve the peaches warm, topped with sour cream and ground cinnamon.

Prep: 25 minutes
Freeze: Up to 4 months
Bake: 50 to 55 minutes

1 cup parboiled (converted) rice (see page 179)
½ cup sliced green onion
6 skinless, boneless chicken breast halves (about 1¼ pounds)
1 teaspoon dried Italian seasoning, crushed
½ teaspoon bottled minced garlic or 1 clove garlic, minced
1 tablespoon cooking oil

1 tablespoon cornstarch
2¼ cups milk
1 3-ounce package cream cheese, cut up
1½ cups loose-pack frozen cut broccoli
½ cup grated Parmesan cheese
⅓ cup diced fully cooked ham
2 tablespoons toasted sliced almonds

1 Cook rice according to package directions; remove from heat and stir in half the onion. Rinse chicken; pat dry with paper towels.

2 In a large skillet cook chicken, Italian seasoning, and garlic in hot oil over medium heat for 8 to 10 minutes or till chicken no longer is pink, turning once. Remove from skillet; reserve drippings.

3 For sauce, cook remaining onion in reserved skillet drippings till tender, adding more oil as necessary. Stir in cornstarch; add milk all at once. Cook and stir over medium heat till slightly thickened and bubbly. Reduce heat; stir in cream cheese till nearly smooth. Remove from heat; stir in broccoli, Parmesan cheese, and ham. Cool.

4 Spread rice in a greased 2-quart rectangular baking dish. Arrange chicken atop rice; season with salt and pepper. Spoon sauce over chicken*. Cover pan with foil; seal, label, and freeze for up to 4 months.

5 The night before serving, place frozen casserole, covered, in the refrigerator to thaw. Bake thawed casserole, covered, in a 350° oven for 30 minutes. Uncover and sprinkle with almonds. Bake for 20 to 25 minutes more or till heated through. Makes 6 servings.

*Note: To assemble, then serve this dish immediately, bake the casserole, covered, in a 350° oven about 10 minutes or till heated through. Sprinkle with almonds.

Per serving: 409 calories, 16 g total fat (7 g saturated), 81 mg cholesterol, 384 mg sodium, 34 g carbohydrate, 1 g fiber, 31 g protein.
Daily Values: 25% vitamin A, 24% vitamin C, 36% calcium, 17% iron.

TURKEY APRICOT STIR-FRY

¾ pound turkey breast tenderloin
  steaks (about 3 steaks)
1 small red sweet pepper, cut into
  1-inch pieces
1 small onion, chopped
½ cup apricot or peach nectar
3 tablespoons soy sauce
2 tablespoons rice vinegar or white
  vinegar

1 tablespoon cornstarch
¼ teaspoon ground red pepper
½ cup dried apricot halves, cut in half
1 cup couscous or long grain rice
1 tablespoon cooking oil
1 6-ounce package frozen pea pods

1 Rinse turkey; pat dry with paper towels. Cut turkey into bite-size strips. Transfer to a storage container. In another storage container combine sweet pepper and onion. For sauce, in a third storage container stir together nectar, soy sauce, vinegar, cornstarch, and ground red pepper; add apricots. Cover and chill all containers for 2 to 24 hours.

2 When ready to serve, prepare couscous or rice according to package directions. Meanwhile, in a wok or large skillet stir-fry sweet pepper mixture in hot oil for 2 to 3 minutes or till crisp-tender. Remove vegetables from pan. (Add more oil as necessary during cooking.) Add the turkey to wok or skillet. Stir-fry for 2 to 3 minutes or till no longer pink. Push turkey from center of pan.

3 Stir sauce and add to center of wok or skillet. Cook and stir over medium heat till thickened and bubbly. Return cooked vegetables to wok; stir in pea pods. Cook and stir about 1 minute more or till pea pods are heated through. Serve immediately over couscous or rice. Makes 4 servings.

Per serving: 387 calories, 6 g total fat (1 g saturated), 37 mg cholesterol, 816 mg sodium, 59 g carbohydrate, 10 g fiber, 25 g protein.
Daily Values: 22% vitamin A, 85% vitamin C, 7% calcium, 25% iron.

When you have time to fix a meal ahead, fix dessert, too. This Rhubarb-Berry Ice is a refreshing finish to the stir-fry meal: In a medium saucepan stir together one 16-ounce package unsweetened sliced rhubarb, 1 cup sugar, and ½ cup cranberry juice cocktail. Bring to boiling; reduce heat. Cover and simmer for 5 to 8 minutes or till rhubarb is tender and sugar is dissolved. Remove from heat. Add another ¾ cup cranberry juice cocktail; cool. In a blender container blend rhubarb mixture, half at a time, till smooth. Transfer to a 1- or 2-quart ice cream freezer and freeze according to manufacturer's directions. Spoon into a freezer container; label and freeze for up to 1 month.

Prep: 25 minutes
Chill: 2 to 24 hours
Cook: 15 minutes

SORTA-LIKE-STUFFED PEPPERS

1½ cups cooked barley or rice, cooled
½ cup finely chopped onion
2 teaspoons instant chicken bouillon
granules
½ teaspoon dried thyme or marjoram,
crushed
¼ teaspoon pepper

1 pound ground turkey
1 medium green sweet pepper, cut
into ¾-inch pieces
1 8-ounce can tomato sauce
Few drops bottled hot pepper sauce
Green sweet pepper rings (optional)

You can use pearl barley or quick-cooking barley for this recipe. If using pearl barley, cook ½ cup barley in 2 cups water, covered, about 45 minutes; drain off any excess liquid. If using quick-cooking barley, cook 1 cup barley in 1½ cups water, covered, for 10 to 12 minutes. Both barleys can be cooked, then covered and chilled for a day or two before you assemble the casserole.

Prep: 25 minutes
Chill: 2 to 24 hours
Bake: 50 to 55 minutes

1 In a large bowl combine cooked barley or rice, onion, bouillon granules, thyme or marjoram, and pepper. Add turkey; mix well.

2 Spread half of the meat mixture in a 2-quart round or square baking dish. Top with sweet pepper pieces. Combine tomato sauce and hot pepper sauce; pour about half of the sauce over sweet pepper. Spread remaining meat mixture in dish*. Cover dish with plastic wrap; chill for 2 to 24 hours. Cover and chill remaining sauce.

3 When ready to serve, bake casserole, uncovered, in a 350° oven for 45 minutes. Using a bulb baster, carefully remove excess juices from dish. Pour remaining sauce over top; bake for 5 to 10 minutes more or till cooked through. Garnish with additional sweet pepper, if desired. Makes 4 servings.

*Note: To assemble, then serve the casserole immediately, bake for 40 minutes, then add the remaining tomato sauce and bake 5 to 10 minutes more.

Per serving: 246 calories, 9 g total fat (2 g saturated), 42 mg cholesterol, 829 mg sodium, 24 g carbohydrate, 18 g protein.
Daily Values: 6% vitamin A, 30% vitamin C, 3% calcium, 18% iron.

CHILI TURKEY LOAVES

2 4-ounce cans whole green chili
   peppers
4 ounces sharp cheddar or Monterey
   Jack cheese
2 beaten eggs
½ cup fine dry bread crumbs
½ cup finely chopped onion
⅓ cup tomato sauce
1 teaspoon dried oregano, crushed
1 teaspoon chili powder

½ teaspoon bottled minced garlic or
   1 clove garlic, minced
½ teaspoon salt
2 pounds ground turkey
1 7- or 8¾-ounce whole-kernel corn,
   drained
   Shredded cheddar or Monterey
   Jack cheese (1 cup)
   Bottled salsa

When ready to dish up this Southwest-inspired entrée, heat a can of black beans, stirring in chopped seeded fresh tomato just before serving. Top with snipped fresh chives.

Prep: 25 minutes
Freeze: Up to 4 months
Bake: 57 minutes

1 Drain peppers and remove seeds. If necessary, cut up peppers to create 8 equal portions. Cut unshredded cheese into eight 3x½x½-inch sticks. In a large bowl combine eggs, bread crumbs, onion, tomato sauce, oregano, chili powder, garlic, and salt. Add turkey; mix well.

2 Divide turkey mixture into 8 portions; form each into a 6x4-inch rectangle. In centers, place some of the corn, one portion of chili peppers, and a cheese stick. Roll up each rectangle from a short side; seal*.

3 Place loaves, seam side down, on a tray lined with waxed paper; freeze. Wrap frozen loaves individually in foil; seal, label, and return to freezer for up to 4 months.

4 When ready to serve, unwrap frozen loaf or loaves and place in a baking pan. Bake, covered, in a 350° oven for 45 minutes. Uncover; bake 10 minutes more or till no longer pink. Spoon off fat. Top each loaf with 2 tablespoons of the shredded cheese; bake 2 minutes more or till melted. Serve with salsa. Makes 8 servings.

*Note: To assemble, then serve immediately, arrange loaf or loaves, seam side down, in a shallow baking pan. Bake, uncovered, in a 350° oven for 30 minutes or till no longer pink. Spoon off fat. Top with shredded cheese; bake 2 minutes more. Serve with salsa.

Per serving: 326 calories, 20 g total fat (9 g saturated), 125 mg cholesterol, 562 mg sodium, 12 g carbohydrate, 1 g fiber, 25 g protein.
Daily Values: 19% vitamin A, 21% vitamin C, 30% calcium, 15% iron.

TURKEY AND DRESSING LOAF

Just before the turkey comes out of the oven, fix instant mashed potatoes and heat up a jar of turkey gravy (look for the newer lower-fat varieties). Add your favorite vegetable or salad side dish.

Prep: 15 minutes
Freeze: Up to 4 months
Bake: 45 to 50 minutes

2 eggs or 3 egg whites, beaten	2 teaspoons poultry seasoning
1½ cups herb-seasoned stuffing croutons	½ teaspoon salt
½ cup finely chopped onion	¼ teaspoon pepper
½ cup finely chopped celery	2 pounds ground turkey
⅓ cup milk or water	1 8-ounce can whole cranberry sauce

1 In a bowl combine eggs, stuffing croutons, onion, celery, milk or water, poultry seasoning, salt, and pepper. Add ground turkey; mix well.

2 Shape meat mixture into 2 loaves; place in two 8x4x2-inch loaf pans*. Cover pans with foil; seal, label, and freeze up to 4 months.

3 When ready to serve, allow frozen loaf or loaves to thaw overnight in the refrigerator. Bake, uncovered, in a 350° oven for 45 to 50 minutes.

4 Stir cranberry sauce and spoon a small amount over meat when 10 minutes baking time remains. In saucepan heat the remaining sauce (use half for each loaf); pass with loaf or loaves. Makes 8 servings total (4 per loaf).

*Note: To assemble, then serve immediately, bake as directed above.

Per serving: 276 calories, 11 g total fat (3 g saturated), 96 mg cholesterol, 436 mg sodium, 26 g carbohydrate, 1 g fiber, 19 g protein.
Daily Values: 3% vitamin A, 4% vitamin C, 5% calcium, 15% iron.

LAMB MUSHROOM LOAF

8 ounces fresh mushrooms
1 medium onion, cut up
2 cloves garlic, quartered, or
   ½ teaspoon garlic powder
1 beaten egg
¼ cup milk
¼ cup couscous
2 tablespoons finely snipped fresh
   basil or 1½ teaspoons dried basil,
   crushed

2 teaspoons Worcestershire sauce
1 teaspoon salt
½ teaspoon pepper
2 pounds lean ground lamb or beef
   Sliced fresh mushrooms (optional)

1 In a blender container or food processor bowl, blend or process the 8 ounces of mushrooms, the onion, and garlic till very finely chopped.

2 In a bowl stir together egg, mushroom mixture, milk, uncooked couscous, basil, Worcestershire sauce, salt, and pepper. Add ground lamb; mix well. Shape meat into one large loaf or eight individual loaves.

3 To freeze, wrap loaf or loaves in heavy duty foil. Seal, label, and freeze up to 4 months.

4 A day before serving, place frozen loaf on a plate in the refrigerator. Let stand in refrigerator overnight to thaw.

5 At serving time, remove foil. Place loaf or loaves in a shallow baking pan. If desired, press additional sliced mushrooms on top of meat.

6 Bake in 350° oven for 45 to 50 minutes for the large loaf, 30 to 40 minutes for the individual loaves. Makes 8 servings total.

Per serving: 270 calories, 16 g total fat (7 g saturated), 103 mg cholesterol, 358 mg sodium, 8 g carbohydrate, 1 g fiber, 22 g protein.
Daily Values: 1% vitamin A, 3% vitamin C, 3% calcium, 14% iron.

An easy way to shape perfect meat loaves is to mold the meat in a loaf pan, then invert the loaves onto heavy-duty foil for freezing.

If you have any Browned Mushroom Sauce (see recipe, page 160) stocked in your freezer, serve it over this tasty meat loaf for extra-rich flavor. Or, prepare an envelope of mushroom sauce mix to serve with the meat. Spoon the sauce over slices of meatloaf and toasted French bread. Brighten each dinner plate with a colorful healthful veggie or two.

Prep: 20 minutes
Freeze: Up to 4 months
Bake: 45 to 50 minutes

GLAZED APPLE MEAT LOAF

While the meat loaf stands 10 minutes before serving, halve and thinly slice a small onion. Cook a 9-ounce package frozen French-cut green beans with the onion and some instant chicken bouillon granules according to the bean package directions. Drain. Dot with margarine; season to taste with a few dashes ground cumin or chili powder.

Prep: 20 minutes
Freeze: Up to 4 months
Bake: 1 to 1¼ hours

2 **beaten eggs**
1 **cup quick-cooking rolled oats**
1 **medium apple, cored and finely chopped (1 cup)**
½ **cup apple juice**
½ **cup chopped onion**
¼ **cup raisins, finely snipped**
1 **teaspoon salt**

1 **teaspoon bottled minced garlic or 2 cloves garlic, minced**
½ **teaspoon pepper**
½ **teaspoon ground cinnamon**
2 **pounds lean ground beef, pork, lamb, or turkey**
Apple jelly, melted

1 In a large bowl combine beaten eggs, oats, apple, apple juice, onion, raisins, salt, garlic, pepper, and cinnamon. Add ground meat; mix well. Shape into two loaves that will fit into two 7½x3½x2-inch or 8x4x2-inch loaf pans.

2 To freeze, line loaf pans with heavy-duty foil three times the width of the pan. Add meat loaves to pan. Fold foil down over food and seal. Freeze till firm. Then lift the foil-wrapped loaves from the pan. Seal, label, and return loaves to freezer for up to 4 months.

3 A day before serving, remove foil from a frozen loaf; return loaf to the original pan. Cover with plastic wrap. Let stand in refrigerator overnight to thaw.

4 At serving time, remove plastic wrap. Bake meat loaf, uncovered, in a 350° oven for 1 to 1¼ hours for the smaller pan size, 50 to 55 minutes for the larger pan size. Remove meat loaf from pan. Brush tops with 1 to 2 tablespoons apple jelly. Let stand 10 minutes; slice to serve. Makes 8 servings total (4 per loaf).

Per serving: 333 calories, 17 g total fat (6 g saturated), 123 mg cholesterol, 347 mg sodium, 21 g carbohydrate, 2 g fiber, 23 g protein.
Daily Values: 2% vitamin A, 4% vitamin C, 2% calcium, 18% iron.

CITRUS-MARINATED FLANK STEAK

This entrée is so simple, you'll feel like a guest at your own dinner. Marinate the flank steak in half of the Citrus-Spice Marinade, then use the remaining marinade as a gourmet dressing for mixed greens tossed with feta cheese and walnuts.

Prep: 20 minutes
Chill: 6 to 24 hours
Grill: 18 to 22 minutes

1 1- to 1½-pound beef flank steak
1 cup Citrus-Spice Marinade

1 medium orange, sliced
   Crushed peppercorns

1 Score meat on both sides by making diagonal cuts at 1-inch intervals on surface. Place in a plastic bag set in a shallow dish; add marinade and orange slices. Seal bag; turn to coat. Marinate in the refrigerator for 6 to 24 hours, turning bag occasionally.

2 When ready to serve, remove steak from bag, reserving marinade. Grill on an uncovered grill directly over medium coals to desired doneness, allowing 18 to 22 minutes for medium. Turn and brush with reserved marinade halfway through grilling time.

3 To serve, slice meat diagonally across the grain into thin slices. Sprinkle with pepper. Makes 4 to 6 servings.

Citrus-Spice Marinade: In a screwtop jar combine 1 cup *orange juice,* ⅓ cup *lemon juice,* ¼ cup *cooking oil,* 3 tablespoons *Worcestershire sauce,* 1½ teaspoons *bottled minced garlic or 3 cloves garlic* (minced), 1 teaspoon *ground cumin,* ¾ teaspoon *onion powder,* ½ teaspoon *salt,* and ½ teaspoon *pepper.* Cover and shake well to mix. Store in the refrigerator. Makes 2 cups.

Per serving: 224 calories, 12 g total fat (4 g saturated), 53 mg cholesterol, 161 mg sodium, 7 g carbohydrate, 1 g fiber, 22 g protein.
Daily Values: 1% vitamin A, 54% vitamin C, 2% calcium, 16% iron.

BEAN AND BEEF ENCHILADA CASSEROLE

½ **pound lean ground beef**
½ **cup chopped onion**
1 **teaspoon chili powder**
½ **teaspoon ground cumin**
1 **15-ounce can pinto beans, drained and rinsed**
1 **4-ounce can diced green chili peppers**
1 **8-ounce carton dairy sour cream or light sour cream**
2 **tablespoons all-purpose flour**

¼ **teaspoon garlic powder**
8 **6-inch corn tortillas, cut into 1-inch-wide strips**
1 **10-ounce can enchilada sauce or one 10½-ounce can tomato puree**
1 **cup shredded cheddar cheese (4 ounces)**
Cilantro sprigs (optional)
Hot chili peppers (optional)

1 In a 10-inch skillet cook the ground meat, onion, chili powder, and cumin till onions are tender and meat is no longer is pink. Drain off any fat. Cool.

2 Stir pinto beans and undrained chili peppers into meat mixture. Transfer cooled meat mixture to a covered storage container; chill. In a covered storage container stir together the sour cream, flour, and garlic powder till well blended; chill up to 24 hours.

3 When ready to serve, place half of the tortilla strips in the bottom of a shallow 2-quart baking dish. Top with half of the meat mixture, half of the sour cream mixture, and half of the enchilada sauce. Repeat layers.

4 Bake, covered, in a 350° oven for 45 minutes*. Uncover; sprinkle with cheese and bake 5 minutes more. Garnish with cilantro and chili peppers, if desired. Makes 4 servings.

*Note: To assemble, then serve this casserole immediately, reduce the baking time to 30 minutes.

Per serving: 617 calories, 32 g total fat (16 g saturated), 90 mg cholesterol, 1,056 mg sodium, 55 g carbohydrate, 6 g fiber, 30 g protein.
Daily Values: 24% vitamin A, 18% vitamin C, 36% calcium, 48% iron.

A satisfying casserole like this one is a real crowd pleaser. So, the next time you need to tote food to a potluck, double this recipe and bake it in a shallow 3- to 4-quart baking dish, covered, about an hour or till the center is hot. Wrap in towels or newspapers to keep warm during transport. Use the tomato puree when preparing for the crowd so the dish isn't too spicy for the youngsters.

For a crowd or a small family, a quick sidekick to this hearty meal is Spanish rice (available in cans); just heat before serving.

Prep: 20 minutes
Chill: Up to 24 hours
Bake: 50 minutes

 PORK

COUNTRY RIBS AND KRAUT

When preparing this meal the day before, there's a good chance the wonderful aroma wafting through your home may convince you to serve the ribs for dinner that day. If so, just skip the reheating step. If you have the willpower to stick with your original plan, however, and save the ribs for the next day, be sure to divide the hot mixture into two smaller dishes. This ensures safe, fast cooling.

Prep: 25 minutes
Bake: 1 to 1½ hours
Chill: Up to 24 hours
Bake: 30 to 35 minutes

2 to 2½ pounds pork country-style ribs (4 ribs)
3 large tart apples, cored and cut into wedges (about 6 cups)
1 16-ounce can sauerkraut, rinsed and drained
2 cups shredded red cabbage
1 cup chopped onion
¼ cup chicken broth
¼ cup packed brown sugar
½ teaspoon caraway seed
¼ teaspoon salt
¼ teaspoon ground nutmeg or allspice
⅛ teaspoon pepper
Dash ground cloves

1 Arrange ribs in a single layer in a shallow roasting pan. Broil 5 to 6 inches from heat for 20 minutes, turning frequently or till browned. Drain well.

2 In a 3-quart rectangular baking dish combine apples, sauerkraut, cabbage, onion, broth, brown sugar, caraway seed, salt, nutmeg, pepper, and cloves. Season ribs with additional salt and pepper, if desired. Place ribs on top of sauerkraut mixture, pushing ribs down into the mixture. Cover tightly with foil.

3 Bake in a 325° oven for 1 to 1½ hours or till meat is tender. Remove from oven. Cool. Divide mixture into two 1½- or 2-quart rectangular baking dishes.

4 Cover the dishes with foil; chill for up to 24 hours.

5 When ready to serve, reheat, covered, in a 350° oven for 30 to 35 minutes or till hot. Spoon juices over ribs. Serve with a slotted spoon. Makes 4 servings.

Per serving: 536 calories, 31 g total fat (12 g saturated), 119 mg cholesterol, 1,062 mg sodium, 35 g carbohydrate, 7 g fiber, 31 g protein.
Daily Values: 1% vitamin A, 67% vitamin C, 10% calcium, 29% iron.

MIX-AND-MATCH MARINARA

1 cup chopped onion
1 teaspoon bottled minced garlic or
   2 large cloves garlic, minced
1 tablespoon olive oil or cooking oil
1 28-ounce can tomatoes, cut up
2 tablespoons tomato paste
1 teaspoon sugar
1 teaspoon dried Italian seasoning,
   crushed

¼ teaspoon salt
  Dash pepper
8 ounces corkscrew pasta or elbow
   macaroni
2 teaspoons olive oil or cooking oil
  Desired mix-and-match options
   (see right)
  Oregano sprigs (optional)

1 In a medium saucepan cook the onion and garlic in the 1 tablespoon hot oil till tender but not brown. Stir in undrained tomatoes, tomato paste, sugar, Italian seasoning, salt, and pepper. Bring to boiling; reduce heat. Simmer, uncovered, for 30 minutes or to desired consistency, stirring occasionally.

2 Meanwhile, cook pasta according to package directions. Drain and toss with the 2 teaspoons oil. Divide pasta among four 1-pint freezer containers. Seal and label.

3 Ladle the sauce into four small freezer containers. Stir one or two desired mix-and-match options into each sauce container. Seal and label. Freeze sauce and pasta for up to 6 months.

4 When ready to serve, transfer 1 container frozen sauce to a small saucepan. Cook over medium-low heat about 10 minutes or till thawed and heated through, stirring occasionally. Meanwhile, in a medium saucepan bring 1 quart water to boiling. Add frozen pasta. Cook for 2 to 3 minutes or just till heated through. Drain thoroughly.

  To reheat 1 serving in the microwave: Transfer 1 container frozen sauce and 1 container frozen pasta into 2 separate microwave-safe containers. Cover each container. Micro-cook sauce on 70% power (medium-high) for 3 minutes. Stir sauce and add the pasta container to the microwave oven. Cook sauce and pasta for 2 to 3 minutes on medium-high or till heated through, stirring pasta once. Garnish with oregano sprigs, if desired. Makes 4 servings pasta and sauce.

Per serving (with chicken and corn): 435 calories, 10 g total fat (2 g saturated), 31 mg cholesterol, 690 mg sodium, 67 mg carbohydrate, 3 g fiber, 21 g protein.
Daily Values: 20% vitamin A, 68% vitamin C, 12% calcium, 32% iron.

These frozen single-serving pasta meals are perfect when family members operate on individual schedules. Tailor-make each serving by stirring one or two of these mix-and-match options into each sauce portion before freezing:

- ¼ cup cooked quartered artichoke heart
- ⅓ cup drained canned garbanzo or black beans
- ¼ cup chopped cooked chicken or ham
- ¼ cup frozen peas, whole kernel corn, or canned sliced mushrooms
- 2 tablespoons chopped pepperoni or crumbled cooked bacon
- 1 tablespoon sliced ripe olives

  Let family members complete the meal with their own side dishes—salad, fruit, or vegetables.

Prep: 45 minutes
Freeze: Up to 6 months
Cook: 10 minutes

MACARONI AND CHEESE PRIMAVERA

Leftover vegetables looking lonely in the refrigerator? Then use them in place of the frozen vegetables called for in the recipe (you'll need about 3 cups cooked vegetables total). Another quick substitute: Try 1½ cups cornflakes in place of the crumb topper.

A platter of assorted mixed fruits is an easy companion to this family-pleasing dish.

Prep: 35 minutes
Freeze: Up to 4 months
Bake: 45 to 50 minutes

1 16-ounce package frozen cauliflower, broccoli, and carrots
6 ounces pasta such as bow ties, corkscrew macaroni, or elbow macaroni
1¼ cups milk
1 teaspoon dry mustard
1 teaspoon Worcestershire sauce
¼ teaspoon bottled hot pepper sauce
8 ounces sharp American cheese, cut into small cubes or shredded
4 ounces process Swiss cheese slices, torn or shredded

1 4-ounce can sliced mushrooms, drained (optional)
2 cups soft bread crumbs (about 2½ slices)
2 tablespoons grated Parmesan cheese
½ teaspoon paprika
2 tablespoons margarine or butter, melted
Snipped fresh parsley (optional)

1 Cook vegetables and pasta separately according to package directions; do not overcook. Drain each well.

2 Return pasta to hot pan. Stir in milk, mustard, Worcestershire sauce, and hot pepper sauce. Bring to boiling; remove from heat. Add American and Swiss cheeses, stirring to melt. Cool.

3 Place cooked vegetables and, if desired, mushrooms on the bottom of an ungreased 2-quart rectangular baking dish. Spoon macaroni and cheese on top of vegetables. For crumb topper, combine bread crumbs, Parmesan cheese, and paprika. Stir in margarine till combined. Sprinkle on top of casserole*. Cover with foil; seal, label, and freeze up to 4 months. (Or, cover with plastic wrap and and refrigerate for up to 24 hours.)

4 When ready to serve, if frozen let thaw in refrigerator overnight. Remove foil or plastic wrap. Bake, uncovered, in a 350° oven for 45 to 50 minutes or till heated through and golden brown. Sprinkle with parsley, if desired. Makes 6 servings.

*Note: To assemble, then serve this dish immediately, bake the casserole, uncovered, in a 350° oven for 30 to 40 minutes or till heated through.

Per serving: 414 calories, 19 g total fat (10 g saturated), 43 mg cholesterol, 990 mg sodium, 41 g carbohydrate, 2 g fiber, 19 g protein.
Daily Values: 52% vitamin A, 49% vitamin C, 40% calcium, 14% iron.

CHEESY RICE AND BARLEY CASSEROLE

2 beaten eggs
2 cups cooked brown or long grain rice
1½ cups cream-style cottage cheese
1 11-ounce can whole-kernel corn with sweet peppers, drained
1¼ cups milk

½ cup quick-cooking barley
1 4-ounce can diced green chili peppers, drained
1 cup shredded cheddar cheese (4 ounces)
1 tomato, seeded and chopped (optional)

1 In a mixing bowl combine eggs, cooked rice, cottage cheese, corn with sweet peppers, milk, uncooked barley, chili peppers, and half of the cheddar cheese. Mix well. Pour into a lightly greased shallow 2-quart baking dish or casserole; sprinkle with remaining cheese.

2 Cover with plastic wrap; chill for 2 to 24 hours.

3 To serve, bake, uncovered, in a 350° oven for 40 to 50 minutes or till a knife inserted near the center comes out clean. Let stand 10 minutes before serving. Sprinkle with tomato, if desired. Makes 6 servings.

Per serving: 354 calories, 13 g total fat (7 g saturated), 103 mg cholesterol, 616 mg sodium, 41 g carbohydrate, 5 g fiber, 20 g protein.
Daily Values: 17% vitamin A, 24% vitamin C, 23% calcium, 12% iron.

To fix enough rice for this dish, you need to prepare ⅔ cup uncooked brown rice according to package directions. But why not just cook up a big batch of rice instead? Use 2 cups of the cooked rice for this recipe and, within a few days, reheat the rest in the microwave oven to serve with a stir-fry or saucy meat mixture.

All this one-step meal needs is a light side-dish. Rather than garnishing the casserole with chopped tomato in the summer, slice several fresh tomatoes to serve on the side. In winter, pass a bowl of marinated vegetable salad.

Prep: 20 minutes
Chill: 2 to 24 hours
Bake: 40 to 50 minutes

CHUNKY TOMATO SOUP WITH SEAFOOD

Keep some "souper" toppers on hand to jazz up soups and stews. Freeze shredded cheese to sprinkle over bean or vegetable soups, and enliven chowders with seasoned croutons, which you also can keep in the freezer.

Don't forget a pantry staple: popcorn. Kids love popped popcorn on their soup; pop the corn while heating the soup, and sprinkle it on top of each serving. Pour glasses of ice cold milk to complete the meal.

Prep: 45 minutes
Freeze: Up to 6 months
Cook: 18 to 25 minutes

1 large onion, chopped	1 bay leaf
2 teaspoons bottled minced garlic or 4 cloves garlic, minced	1½ pounds potatoes, cut up (about 4 cups)
1 tablespoon cooking oil or olive oil	2 carrots, thinly sliced
2 16-ounce cans diced tomatoes	2 medium green sweet peppers, cut into 1-inch squares
1½ cups dry white wine or 1½ cups chicken broth plus 1 tablespoon lemon juice	1 stalk celery, sliced
1 cup clam juice	2 8-ounce portions frozen cod, orange roughy, snapper, haddock, or halibut
1 teaspoon dried oregano, crushed	2 8-ounce portions frozen peeled and deveined shrimp or scallops
½ teaspoon dried thyme, crushed	
⅛ to ¼ teaspoon ground red pepper	

1 In a 4½-quart Dutch oven cook onion and garlic in hot oil for 1 minute. Stir in undrained tomatoes, wine or broth, clam juice, oregano, thyme, ground red pepper, and bay leaf. Add potatoes, carrots, sweet peppers, and celery.

2 Bring to boiling; reduce heat. Cover and simmer for 20 to 25 minutes or till vegetables are tender. Discard bay leaf. Cool.

3 Divide mixture into two covered storage or freezer containers. Seal, label, and freeze for up to 6 months.

4 When ready to serve, thaw one portion each of fish and shrimp or scallops. Transfer one portion of soup to a 2-quart saucepan. Cook, covered, over medium-low heat about 15 to 20 minutes or till hot and bubbly, stirring occasionally. Add thawed fish and shrimp or scallops. Cover and cook for 3 to 5 minutes more or till fish flakes and shrimp or scallops are opaque. Serve in bowls. Makes 8 servings (two 4-serving portions).

Per serving: 276 calories, 3 g total fat (1 g saturated), 88 mg cholesterol, 544 mg sodium, 36 g carbohydrate, 3 g fiber, 21 g protein.
Daily Values: 41% vitamin A, 81% vitamin C, 7% calcium, 28% iron.

THREE BEAN AND BEEF STEW

8 ounces boneless beef chuck, cut into 1-inch cubes
1 cup chopped onion
1 teaspoon bottled minced garlic or 2 cloves garlic, minced
1 tablespoon cooking oil
2 cups water
1 16-ounce can diced tomatoes
½ cup dry red wine or 3 tablespoons red wine vinegar plus ⅓ cup water
⅓ cup tomato paste
¼ cup snipped fresh basil or 1 tablespoon dried basil, crushed

1 tablespoon brown sugar
1 teaspoon dry mustard
¾ teaspoon salt
¼ teaspoon pepper
4 carrots, cut into ¼-inch slices
1 15-ounce can black beans, rinsed and drained
1 15-ounce can great northern or navy beans, rinsed and drained
1 9-ounce package frozen Italian-style green beans
Fresh basil sprigs (optional)

Try this zesty bread along with your Italian-style soup: Brush 6-inch Italian bread shells (Boboli brand) with olive oil, then top with thinly sliced onions that have been cooked in a little cooking oil till brown. Sprinkle crumbled blue cheese over all. Bake bread shells in a hot oven about 10 minutes or till heated through. Cut into wedges to serve.

Prep: 20 minutes
Cook: 1¼ hours
Freeze: Up to 3 months
Cook: 30 minutes

1 In a 4½-quart Dutch oven brown beef cubes with onion and garlic in hot oil till meat is brown and onion is tender.

2 Stir in water, undrained tomatoes, wine, tomato paste, the ¼ cup snipped basil, brown sugar, dry mustard, salt, and pepper. Stir in carrots. Bring to boiling; reduce heat. Cover and simmer 1¼ hours*. Stir in canned beans.

3 Set Dutch oven in a sink of ice water to chill quickly; stir stew occasionally. Transfer mixture to two 1½-quart freezer containers. Seal, label, and freeze up to 3 months.

4 When ready to serve, transfer one portion of frozen stew to a large sauce-pan. Cover and cook over medium heat about 20 minutes or till heated through, stirring occasionally to break up mixture. Stir in half of the green beans; bring to boiling. Reduce heat; simmer, covered, about 10 minutes or till beans are tender. Serve in bowls; garnish with a sprig of basil, if desired. Makes 6 servings (two 3-serving portions).

*Note: To prepare and serve this soup immediately, after the 1¼ hours cook-ing time, stir in the whole package of green beans. Simmer 8 to 10 minutes more or till meat and beans are tender. Stir in canned beans and heat through. Leftovers may be frozen.

Per serving: 337 calories, 7 g total fat (2 g saturated), 38 mg cholesterol, 994 mg sodium, 45 g carbohydrate, 8 g fiber, 26 g protein.
Daily Values: 124% vitamin A, 41% vitamin C, 11% calcium, 36% iron.

PORK AND LENTIL SOUP

10 cups water
 8 ounces lean boneless pork, cut into
       ½-inch cubes
 2 cups chopped onion
1½ cups chopped carrot
1⅓ cups lentils, rinsed and drained
 1 cup chopped celery with leaves
 2 tablespoons instant beef bouillon
       granules

1½ teaspoons dried marjoram, crushed
 1 teaspoon dried basil, crushed
 ¼ teaspoon pepper
 ⅛ teaspoon ground cumin
 1 bay leaf
 1 6-ounce can tomato paste
       Crisp-cooked bacon, coarsely
       chopped (3 to 4 slices)

To complete this healthful dinner, toss a spinach salad with bits of roasted sweet pepper and toasted walnuts. Drizzle with poppy seed dressing, if desired, and serve with the soup.

When freezing foods, always label them—otherwise, you can end up with mystery packages buried in the back of the freezer. You can use a crayon, pen, or waterproof marking pen or pencil to label foods. Be sure to include the date and contents and any other information you think is pertinent (special cooking instructions, for instance).

Prep: 50 minutes
Freeze: Up to 3 months
Cook: 35 to 40 minutes

1 In a 4½-quart Dutch oven combine all ingredients except tomato paste and bacon. Bring to boiling; reduce heat. Cover and simmer for 20 minutes. Remove from heat. Remove bay leaf. Stir in tomato paste*. Cool.

2 Transfer soup to two 2-quart freezer containers. Seal, label, and freeze up to 3 months.

3 When ready to serve, transfer one portion of frozen soup to a large saucepan. Cover and cook over medium heat for 35 to 40 minutes or till bubbly, stirring occasionally to break up mixture. Sprinkle bacon over each serving. Makes 8 servings (two 4-serving portions).

***Note:** To prepare, then serve this soup immediately, stir the cooked bacon into soup with the tomato paste. Continue to cook, covered, for 10 minutes more (30 minutes total) or till lentils and vegetables are tender. Leftovers may be frozen.

Per serving: 204 calories, 4 g total fat (1 g saturated), 15 mg cholesterol, 760 mg sodium, 30 g carbohydrate, 4 g fiber, 15 g protein.
Daily Values: 69% vitamin A, 26% vitamin C, 5% calcium, 27% iron.

SAUSAGE-VEGETABLE SOUP

1 pound bulk Italian sausage

2 14½-ounce cans beef or vegetable broth

2 14½-ounce cans Italian-style stewed tomatoes

1½ cups water

1 15-ounce can cannellini or red kidney beans, rinsed and drained

3 potatoes, cut into ½-inch cubes (3 cups)

3 celery stalks, sliced (1½ cups)

1 large onion, cut into thin wedges

1 teaspoon bottled minced garlic or 2 cloves garlic, minced

1 small zucchini, halved lengthwise and sliced

1 In a 4½-quart Dutch oven cook the sausage till crumbly and browned. Drain off the fat.

2 Add broth, undrained tomatoes, water, beans, potatoes, celery, onion, and garlic. Bring to boiling; reduce heat. Cover and simmer for 25 minutes. Stir in zucchini*. Remove from heat. Cool.

3 Transfer mixture to two 2-quart freezer containers. Seal, label, and freeze up to 3 months.

4 When ready to serve, transfer one portion of frozen soup to a large sauce-pan. Cover and cook over medium heat about 30 minutes or till hot, stirring occasionally to break up mixture. Makes 8 servings (two 4-serving portions).

***Note:** To prepare, then serve immediately, cook the soup for 5 minutes more after adding zucchini. Leftovers may be frozen.

Per serving: 232 calories, 9 g total fat (3 g saturated), 22 mg cholesterol, 1,155 mg sodium, 30 g carbohydrate, 4 g fiber, 12 g protein.
Daily Values: 8% vitamin A, 33% vitamin C, 5% calcium, 11% iron.

For even heartier fare on a cold winter night, serve a variety of cheeses and crackers with this comforting soup. Full-flavored cheeses such as sharp cheddar, Asiago, gouda (try the smoked variety), and Gruyère are perfect complements. Cheese tastes best when served at room temperature, so let your selections sit out while the soup simmers.

Prep: 45 minutes
Freeze: Up to 3 months
Cook: 30 minutes

MINESTRONE

6 cups water
1 28-ounce can tomatoes, cut up
1 8-ounce can tomato sauce
1 large onion, chopped
1 cup chopped cabbage
1 medium carrot, chopped
1 stalk celery, chopped
4 teaspoons instant beef bouillon
 granules
1 tablespoon dried Italian seasoning,
 crushed
1 teaspoon bottled minced garlic or
 2 cloves garlic, minced

¼ teaspoon pepper
1 15-ounce can cannellini or great
 northern beans
1 10-ounce package frozen lima
 beans or one 9-ounce package
 frozen Italian-style green beans
4 ounces broken linguini or
 spaghetti
1 small zucchini, halved lengthwise
 and sliced
2 to 3 tablespoons purchased pesto
 (optional)
 Grated Parmesan cheese

1 In a 5- to 6-quart Dutch oven combine water, undrained tomatoes, tomato sauce, onion, cabbage, carrot, celery, bouillon granules, Italian seasoning, garlic, and pepper. Bring to boiling; reduce heat.

2 Cover and simmer for 10 minutes. Stir in undrained cannellini or great northern beans, lima beans, linguini, and zucchini. Return to boiling; reduce heat. Simmer, uncovered, for 15 minutes. Remove from heat. Cool.

3 Transfer soup to two 2-quart freezer containers. Seal, label, and freeze up to 3 months.

4 When ready to serve, transfer one portion of frozen soup to a large saucepan. Cover and cook over medium heat for 25 to 30 minutes or till heated through, stirring occasionally to break up mixture. Serve in bowls; top each serving with 1 teaspoon pesto, if desired. Pass Parmesan cheese to sprinkle over soup. Makes 8 servings (two 4-serving portions).

Per serving: 177 calories, 3 g total fat (1 g saturated), 5 mg cholesterol, 992 mg sodium, 32 g carbohydrate, 5 g fiber, 10 g protein.
Daily Values: 33% vitamin A, 41% vitamin C, 14% calcium, 19% iron.

While the soup reheats, set out an antipasto tray that includes a variety of cold cuts, such as salami and ham, cheese slices or cubes, green olives, ripe olives, pickled peppers, marinated artichoke hearts, and fresh vegetable sticks.

For a sweet fruit to complement the flavors of the savory foods, try strawberries, cantaloupe or honeydew melon, and figs.

Prep: 50 minutes
Freeze: Up to 3 months
Cook: 25 to 30 minutes

SASSY BEEF IN TORTILLAS

Don't panic if you're out of tortillas when you pull the meat sauce out of the freezer. It also tastes great served over baked potatoes, spaghetti, or spaghetti squash. When the sauce is wrapped in tortillas, serve with canned spanish rice. When the sauce is spooned over potatoes, include a fruit salad side-dish. A marinated vegetable salad from the deli complements the sauce when served over spaghetti.

Prep: 40 minutes
Freeze: Up to 3 months
Cook: 15 to 20 minutes

2 **pounds lean ground beef, pork, chicken, or turkey**	⅓ **cup light raisins**
1 **cup chopped onion**	⅓ **cup catsup**
1½ **cups shredded carrot or butternut squash**	3 **tablespoons steak sauce**
1 **cup finely chopped green sweet pepper**	2 **tablespoons quick-cooking barley**
1 **14½-ounce can diced tomatoes**	1 **tablespoon chili powder**
1 **8-ounce can tomato sauce**	¼ **teaspoon salt**
	¼ **teaspoon pepper**
	15 **8- to 9-inch flour tortillas**

1 In a 4½-quart Dutch oven cook ground meat and onion till meat no longer is pink and onion is tender. Drain off fat.

2 Stir in carrot or squash, sweet pepper, undrained tomatoes, tomato sauce, raisins, catsup, steak sauce, barley, chili powder, salt, and pepper. Bring to boiling; reduce heat.

3 Cover and simmer for 10 minutes. Uncover; cook for 10 to 15 minutes more or till mixture is desired consistency. Remove from heat. Cool.

4 Transfer mixture to 1- or 2-cup freezer containers. Seal, label, and freeze up to 3 months.

5 When ready to serve, transfer 1 container of the frozen sauce to a small or medium saucepan. Cook, covered, over medium-low heat 15 to 20 minutes or till thawed and heated through, stirring occasionally.

  To reheat in the microwave: Transfer frozen mixture to a microwave-safe bowl. Micro-cook on 70% power (medium-high), stirring occasionally; allow 6 minutes for 1 cup mixture or 10 to 11 minutes for 2 cups.

6 Spoon about ½ cup of the meat mixture over half of a warm tortilla. Fold in half and then in half again. Makes 15 servings (7½ cups).

Per serving: 279 calories, 10 g total fat (3 g saturated), 38 mg cholesterol, 505 mg sodium, 31 g carbohydrate, 3 g fiber, 16 g protein.
Daily Values: 36% vitamin A, 19% vitamin C, 5% calcium, 18% iron.

SPICY BEEF PITAS

1 pound thinly sliced cooked beef
½ cup picante sauce
⅓ cup red wine vinegar
¼ cup olive oil or cooking oil
1 tablespoon snipped fresh cilantro
    or parsley
⅛ teaspoon garlic powder

⅛ teaspoon cracked black pepper
4 large pita bread rounds, halved
1 medium tomato, chopped
1 medium avocado, sliced
¼ cup crumbled feta cheese
    (1 ounce)

1 Place sliced beef in a plastic bag set inside a bowl. For marinade, in a medium bowl combine the picante sauce, vinegar, oil, cilantro, garlic powder, and pepper. Pour marinade over beef. Seal bag; marinate in the refrigerator for 4 to 24 hours, turning bag occasionally.

2 When ready to serve, drain and discard marinade. Divide beef among pita bread halves. Add tomato, avocado, and feta cheese. Makes 8 servings.

Per serving: 399 calories, 32 g total fat (10 g saturated), 55 mg cholesterol, 364 mg sodium, 14 g carbohydrate, 1 g fiber, 16 g protein.
Daily Values: 5% vitamin A, 15% vitamin C, 6% calcium, 15% iron.

For a fast, flavorful side dish, cook a package of cheese-stuffed tortellini according to package directions; drain and cool. Toss with sweet pepper strips, red onion slices, ripe olives, and Italian dressing.

Prep: 15 minutes
Chill: 4 to 24 hours
Finish: 15 minutes

FOOD SAFETY TIPS

Follow these tips to ensure the safe handling and storage of your food.
■ Maintain the refrigerator at 36° to 40° and the freezer at 0° or below.
■ Thaw food in the refrigerator overnight or in the microwave oven. Do not thaw food at room temperature.
■ Cook all foods thoroughly. Do not partially cook food, stop, and then finish cooking later.
■ When serving hot foods, hold them for no longer than 2 hours and keep the food between 140° and 165°.
■ Discard chilled food that has been at room temperature for more than 2 hours.
■ Promptly place leftovers in the refrigerator or freezer. A large quantity of hot food should be cooled quickly before refrigerating or freezing it. To do this, place the container in a sink filled with ice water. Or, divide the food into smaller portions before refrigerating or freezing, so it will cool faster.
■ Reheat leftovers thoroughly. Covering helps the food heat evenly. Gravy should come to a rolling boil.

RED HOT BRATS IN BEER

Even on a cold or rainy day, you can make a picnic in your kitchen. Stop by the deli for chilled salads and pick up a bag of chips to serve with these brassy brats.

Prep: 30 minutes
Chill: 4 to 24 hours
Grill: 7 to 8 minutes

6 fresh (uncooked) bratwursts
   (about 1¼ pounds total)
2 12-ounce cans beer
1 tablespoon bottled hot pepper
   sauce
1 tablespoon Worcestershire sauce

2 teaspoons ground red pepper
1 teaspoon chili powder
6 frankfurter buns, split
   Sauerkraut (optional)
   Pickles (optional)
   Mustard (optional)

1 Prick several holes in the skin of each bratwurst. In a Dutch oven or large saucepan combine the bratwursts, beer, hot pepper sauce, Worcestershire sauce, ground red pepper, and chili powder. Bring to boiling; reduce heat. Simmer, covered, about 20 minutes or till brats no longer are pink. Drain; cool. Chill, covered, for 4 to 24 hours.

2 At serving time, grill brats on an uncovered grill directly over medium-hot coals for 7 to 8 minutes or till the bratwurst skins are golden, turning frequently. Serve on buns with sauerkraut, pickles, or mustard, if desired. Or top with Pepper-Pear Relish* (shown in photo, right). Makes 6 servings.

*Note: For a change of taste when dishing up char-grilled brats, serve this sweet and tangy relish in place of the mustard and pickles. Pepper-Pear Relish: In a saucepan combine ¾ cup *cider vinegar,* 1 small *pear* (peeled and finely chopped), 1 *red sweet pepper* (finely chopped), 1 *onion* (finely chopped), one 4-ounce can *diced green chili peppers* (drained), ¼ cup *sugar,* 2 teaspoons *prepared mustard,* and ⅛ teaspoon *ground turmeric.* Bring to boiling, reduce heat. Simmer, uncovered, for 30 minutes. Cool. Cover and chill up to 4 days.

Per serving: 290 calories, 15 g total fat (7 g saturated), 44 mg cholesterol, 1,070 mg sodium, 24 g carbohydrate, 2 g fiber, 13 g protein.
Daily Values; 5% vitamin A, 35% vitamin C, 11% calcium, 11% iron.

TEX-MEX TORTILLA STACK

1 9-ounce package (2 cups) frozen chopped cooked chicken, thawed
1 cup finely chopped peeled jicama
½ cup taco sauce
8 10-inch flour tortillas
1 6-ounce container frozen avocado dip, thawed
2 cups chopped lettuce
1 16-ounce can refried beans with green chili peppers or Mexican-style beans, drained and mashed

1 8-ounce carton light or regular sour cream
⅓ cup chopped red sweet pepper
⅓ cup sliced green onion
1 cup shredded reduced-fat or regular cheddar cheese, Cojack cheese, or Monterey Jack cheese with jalapeño peppers
¼ cup sliced pitted ripe olives
   Taco sauce (optional)

Fresh fruit is the choice to serve with this fun layered sandwich. Toss fresh fruits such as peaches, plums, berries, or whole grapes with a little orange juice spiced with ground cinnamon.

Prep: 30 minutes
Chill: 1 to 3 hours

1 In a medium mixing bowl combine chicken, jicama, and the ½ cup taco sauce; set aside.

2 Place one flour tortilla on a platter; spread with half of the chicken mixture. On a second tortilla, spread half of the avocado dip; place, avocado side up, on top of chicken on first tortilla. Sprinkle with half of the lettuce. Top with a third tortilla; spread with half of the beans. Top with a fourth tortilla; add half each of the sour cream, red pepper, green onion, and cheese.

3 Repeat layers, ending with remaining sour cream, red pepper, green onion, and cheese. Sprinkle with olives. Cover and chill for 1 to 3 hours.

4 When ready to serve, cut into 8 wedges. Pass taco sauce, if desired. Makes 8 servings.

Per serving: 392 calories, 15 g total fat (3 g saturated), 42 mg cholesterol, 566 mg sodium, 42 g carbohydrate, 4 g fiber, 24 g protein.
Daily Values: 13% vitamin A, 26% vitamin C, 29% calcium, 24% iron.

SPINACH SALAD WITH CHICKEN AND FRUIT

This refreshing salad calls for warm bread on the side. Separate a package of refrigerated breadsticks. Uncoil and cut each bread-stick in half. Twist dough. Brush dough with beaten egg, then sprinkle with grated Parmesan cheese. Bake according to package directions.

Prep: 30 minutes
Chill: Up to 24 hours
Finish: 15 minutes

6 cups fresh spinach (8 ounces)
¼ cup salad oil
3 tablespoons red wine vinegar
3 tablespoons orange juice
1 tablespoon Dijon-style mustard
½ teaspoon poppy seeds
1 11-ounce can mandarin oranges, chilled and drained
1½ cups cubed cooked chicken or turkey or two 5-ounce cans chunk-style chicken, drained and flaked
2 cups strawberry halves or cantaloupe cubes

1 Rinse and tear spinach. Cover and store in refrigerator. For dressing, in a screwtop jar combine oil, red wine vinegar, orange juice, mustard, and poppy seeds. Cover and shake well. Chill up to 24 hours.

2 When ready to serve, in a large salad bowl combine spinach, orange sections, chicken, and strawberries or cantaloupe. Shake dressing and drizzle over salad; toss to coat. Makes 4 to 6 servings.

Per serving: 288 calories, 19 g total fat (3 g saturated), 47 mg cholesterol, 207 mg sodium, 14 g carbohydrate, 4 g fiber, 19 g protein.
Daily Values: 58% vitamin A, 146% vitamin C, 10% calcium, 21% iron.

CHICKEN AND CHEDDAR PASTA TOSS

6 ounces no-boil pasta ribbons or
   no-boil lasagna noodles, broken
1 8¼-ounce package frozen mesquite
   grilled chicken tenders or one
   9-ounce package frozen chopped
   cooked chicken, slightly thawed
3 ounces reduced-fat cheddar or
   American cheese, cut into ¾-inch
   cubes

1 green, yellow, or red sweet pepper,
   cut into strips
1 ounce pepperoni, chopped
1 8-ounce bottle nonfat Italian salad
   dressing
⅛ teaspoon cracked black pepper
5 cups torn endive
1 cup red or yellow cherry tomatoes,
   halved

1 In a large mixing bowl cover noodles with boiling water. Let stand for 10 minutes, separating the noodles occasionally with a fork. Drain. Rinse with cold water and drain again. If using chicken tenders, halve them crosswise.

2 Return noodles to mixing bowl; stir in chicken, cheese, sweet pepper, and pepperoni. Add dressing and cracked pepper; toss gently to coat. Cover and chill for 2 to 24 hours.

3 When ready to serve, add endive and tomatoes; toss gently to mix. Makes 6 servings.

Per serving: 252 calories, 7 g total fat (2 g saturated), 36 mg cholesterol, 792 mg sodium, 28 g carbohydrate, 1 g fiber, 19 g protein.
Daily Values: 17% vitamin A, 31% vitamin C, 16% calcium, 8% iron.

Roasted red peppers make a robust topper for French bread or whole-grain crackers to serve with the salad. For sweet red pepper spread, place one 7-ounce jar roasted sweet peppers (drained) in a blender container; blend smooth. Add 2 tablespoons tomato paste, 1 teaspoon sugar, ½ teaspoon garlic powder, ¼ teaspoon each dried thyme (crushed) and salt, and dash ground red pepper. Cover and blend till nearly smooth. Store, covered, in the refrigerator for up to 1 week.

Prep: 20 minutes
Chill: 2 to 24 hours
Finish: 10 minutes

WARM PORK AND LENTIL-RICE SALAD

Besides being crisp and cold, salads today also come warm. In this type of salad, a sautéed piece of meat (such as the pork in this recipe) caps a bed of greens. For an impromptu meal with high style, buy a bag of ready-to-use mixed salad greens and arrange on plates. Then sauté strips of boneless beef sirloin, chicken breasts, or turkey tenderloins till done and place atop greens. Serve with your favorite dressing and croutons, and fresh in-season fruit.

Prep: 30 minutes
Chill: 2 to 24 hours
Finish: 20 minutes

2¼ cups water
½ cup lentils, rinsed and drained
½ cup long grain rice
1 medium carrot, sliced
1 medium onion, chopped
½ teaspoon salt
½ teaspoon dried basil, crushed
¼ teaspoon pepper
¼ cup clear Italian salad dressing

1 teaspoon Dijon-style mustard
1 large tomato, chopped
1 small green sweet pepper, chopped
12 ounces pork tenderloin, cut crosswise into ¼-inch-thick slices
2 tablespoons clear Italian salad dressing
Leaf lettuce leaves

1 In a 1½-quart saucepan combine water, lentils, rice, carrot, onion, salt, basil, and pepper. Bring to boiling; reduce heat. Cover tightly and simmer for 15 to 20 minutes or till rice and lentils are tender. Drain off any excess liquid.

2 Combine the ¼ cup dressing and the mustard; stir into lentil mixture, mixing well. Cover and chill for 2 to 24 hours.

3 When ready to serve, stir tomato and sweet pepper into lentil mixture. In a 10-inch skillet heat 1 tablespoon Italian dressing. Cook half of the pork in hot dressing over medium-high heat for 1 to 2 minutes per side or till done. Remove from skillet; keep warm. Repeat with remaining meat and dressing.

4 Line dinner plates with lettuce leaves; spoon lentil mixture onto lettuce leaves, then top with hot pork slices. Serve immediately. Makes 4 servings.

Per serving: 399 calories, 15 g total fat (3 g saturated), 60 mg cholesterol, 539 mg sodium, 40 g carbohydrate, 3 g fiber, 27 g protein.
Daily Values: 49% vitamin A, 37% vitamin C, 4% calcium, 31% iron.

SHRIMP AND RICE SALAD

1½ cups water
¾ cup brown rice
1½ pounds fresh or frozen shrimp in shells, thawed
2 stalks celery, thinly sliced (1 cup)
¼ cup chopped red or green sweet pepper
2 green onions, sliced
1 8-ounce can sliced water chestnuts, drained

1 small canned jalapeño pepper, rinsed, seeded, and finely chopped (2 to 3 teaspoons) (optional)
¼ cup rice vinegar or white vinegar
2 tablespoons soy sauce
2 tablespoons olive oil or salad oil
1 teaspoon sugar
½ teaspoon toasted sesame oil (optional)
Shredded red cabbage or spinach

1 Bring the 1½ cups water to boiling; add rice. Cover and simmer about 35 minutes or till rice is tender and water is absorbed. Rinse rice with cold water; drain well.

2 Meanwhile, peel and devein shrimp. In a large saucepan bring a large amount of water to boiling. Add shrimp; simmer for 1 to 3 minutes or till shrimp turn pink, stirring occasionally. Drain; rinse with cold water and drain again.

3 In a large bowl combine cooked rice, cooked shrimp, celery, sweet pepper, green onion, water chestnuts, and, if desired, jalapeño pepper. Stir together the vinegar, soy sauce, oil, sugar, and, if desired, sesame oil. Add to shrimp mixture; toss to mix well. Cover and chill for 4 to 24 hours.

4 When ready to serve, fluff rice mixture with a fork; serve over shredded cabbage or spinach. Makes 6 servings.

Per serving: 217 calories, 6 g total fat (1 g saturated), 148 mg cholesterol, 500 mg sodium, 22 g carbohydrate, 2 g fiber, 19 g protein.
Daily Values: 15% vitamin A, 48% vitamin C, 5% calcium, 23% iron.

After a light salad supper, indulge your sweet tooth with a luscious apricot sauce served over scoops of frozen vanilla yogurt. For sauce: In a saucepan combine ¾ cup snipped dried apricots, ¼ teaspoon grated orange peel, and 1¼ cups orange juice. Bring to boiling; reduce heat. Cover and simmer 5 minutes. Stir together ¼ cup sugar and ½ teaspoon cornstarch; stir into saucepan. Cook till thick and bubbly.

Prep: 25 minutes
Chill: 4 to 24 hours
Finish: 10 minutes

LENTIL-RICE SALAD

Crunchy baked tortilla strips make the perfect partner for this salad. Cut corn tortillas into 1-inch-wide strips. Spread strips in a single layer on a baking sheet. Lightly spray the strips with nonstick cooking spray; sprinkle with onion powder and pepper. Bake in a 350° oven for 10 to 12 minutes or till crisp. You can make these ahead and store them in a tightly covered container.

Prep: 40 minutes
Chill: 4 to 24 hours
Finish: 10 minutes

½ cup lentils, rinsed and drained
2 cups water
½ cup long grain rice
½ cup chopped red or green sweet pepper
⅓ cup shredded carrot
¼ cup thinly sliced green onion
3 tablespoons olive oil
½ teaspoon grated lemon peel

3 tablespoons lemon juice
1½ teaspoons fresh snipped basil
¼ teaspoon salt
Lettuce leaves
1 medium tomato, cut into wedges
4 ounces cheddar cheese, sliced
Basil sprigs (optional)

1 In a saucepan combine uncooked lentils and water. Bring to boiling; reduce heat. Simmer, covered, 5 minutes. Add rice. Simmer 15 minutes more. Remove from heat. Let stand, covered, 10 minutes; drain. Rinse with cold water; drain again.

2 Combine lentil-rice mixture, sweet pepper, carrot, and green onion.

3 In a screw-top jar combine oil, lemon peel and juice, basil, and salt. Cover; shake well. Pour over lentil mixture; toss. Cover; chill 4 to 24 hours.

4 When ready to serve, fluff rice mixture with a fork. Serve on lettuce with tomato and cheese. Garnish with basil sprigs, if desired. Makes 4 servings.

Per serving: 386 calories, 20 g total fat (7 g saturated), 30 mg cholesterol, 329 mg sodium, 38 g carbohydrate, 3 g fiber, 14 g protein.
Daily Values: 49% vitamin A, 59% vitamin C, 21% calcium, 24% iron.

Emergency Substitution Chart

EMERGENCY SUBSTITUTIONS

IF YOU DON'T HAVE:	SUBSTITUTE:
1 cup buttermilk	1 tablespoon lemon juice or vinegar plus enough milk to make 1 cup (let stand); or 1 cup yogurt
1 cup light cream	1 tablespoon melted butter plus enough whole milk to make 1 cup
1 cup dairy sour cream	1 cup plain yogurt
1 whole egg	2 egg yolks, 2 egg whites or 3 tablespoons frozen egg product, thawed
1 cup beef broth or chicken broth	1 teaspoon or 1 cube instant beef or chicken bouillon plus 1 cup hot water
1 slice crisp-cooked bacon, crumbled	1 tablespoon cooked bacon pieces
¼ cup fine dry bread crumbs	¾ cup soft bread crumbs or ¼ cup cracker crumbs or ¼ cup cornflake crumbs
2 cups tomato sauce	¾ cup tomato paste plus 1 cup water
1 cup tomato juice	½ cup tomato sauce plus ½ cup water
1 tablespoon cornstarch (for thickening)	2 tablespoons all-purpose flour
1 small onion, chopped (⅓ cup)	1 teaspoon onion powder or 1 tablespoon minced onion, dried
1 clove garlic	½ teaspoon bottled minced garlic or ⅛ teaspoon garlic powder
1 tablespoon poultry seasoning	¾ teaspoon dried sage, crushed; plus ¼ teaspoon dried thyme or marjoram, crushed
1 teaspoon dry mustard	1 tablespoon prepared mustard (in cooked mixtures)
1 tablespoon snipped fresh herb	½ to 1 teaspoon dried herb, crushed
1 teaspoon dried herb	½ teaspoon ground herb
1 teaspoon lemon juice	½ teaspoon vinegar
1 teaspoon grated gingerroot	¼ teaspoon ground ginger

A-C

HOW WE FIGURE NUTRITION INFORMATION

With each recipe, we give important nutrition information. The calorie count of each serving and the amount, in grams, of fat, saturated fat, cholesterol, sodium, carbohydrate, fiber, and protein will help you keep tabs on what you eat.

You can check the levels of each recipe serving for vitamin A, vitamin C, calcium, and iron. These are noted in percentages of the Daily Value. The Daily Values are dietary standards determined by the Food and Drug Administration (FDA).

HOW WE ANALYZE

■ We omit optional ingredients from the nutrition analysis.
■ The analysis is calculated using two-percent milk.
■ When ingredient choices appear in a recipe (such as margarine or butter), we use the first one mentioned for analysis.
■ We use the first serving size listed when a range is given.

WHAT YOU NEED

■ Calories: about 2,000 ■ Cholesterol: less than 300 milligrams
■ Total Fat: less than 65 grams ■ Saturated Fat: less than 20 grams
■ Carbohydrates: about 300 grams ■ Dietary Fiber: 20 to 30 grams
■ Sodium: less than 2,400 milligrams

Use our analyses to chart the nutrition value of the foods you eat. The dietary guidelines above suggest the levels of nutrients that moderately active adults should strive to eat each day. There's no real harm in going over or under these guidelines in any single day, but it is a good idea to aim for a balanced diet over time.

Metric Cooking Hints

By making a few conversions, cooks in Australia, Canada, and the United Kingdom can use the recipes in Better Homes and Gardens® *What's for Dinner?* cookbook with confidence. The charts on this page provide a guide for converting measurements from the U.S. customary system, which is used throughout this book, to the imperial and metric systems. There also is a conversion table for oven temperatures to accommodate the differences in oven calibrations.

Volume and Weight: Americans traditionally use cup measures for liquid and solid ingredients. The chart (top right) shows the approximate imperial and metric equivalents. If you are accustomed to weighing solid ingredients, here are some helpful approximate equivalents.
■ 1 cup butter, caster sugar, or rice = 8 ounces = about 250 grams
■ 1 cup flour = 4 ounces = about 125 grams
■ 1 cup icing sugar = 5 ounces = about 150 grams
   Spoon measures are used for smaller amounts of ingredients. Although the size of the tablespoon varies slightly among countries, for practical purposes and for recipes in this book, a straight substitution is all that's necessary.
   Measurements made using cups or spoons should always be level, unless stated otherwise.

Product Differences: Most of the ingredients called for in the recipes in this book are available in English-speaking countries. However, some are known by different names. Here are some common American ingredients and their possible counterparts:
■ Sugar is granulated or caster sugar.
■ Powdered sugar is icing sugar.
■ All-purpose flour is plain household flour or white flour. When self-rising flour is used in place of all-purpose flour in a recipe that calls for leavening, omit the leavening agent (baking soda or baking powder) and salt.
■ Light corn syrup is golden syrup.
■ Cornstarch is cornflour.
■ Baking soda is bicarbonate of soda.
■ Vanilla is vanilla essence.

Useful Equivalents

⅛ teaspoon = 0.5 ml
¼ teaspoon = 1 ml
½ teaspoon = 2 ml
1 teaspoon = 5 ml
¼ cup = 2 fluid ounces = 50 ml
⅓ cup = 3 fluid ounces = 75 ml
½ cup = 4 fluid ounces = 125 ml
⅔ cup = 5 fluid ounces = 150 ml
¾ cup = 6 fluid ounces = 175 ml
1 cup = 8 fluid ounces = 250 ml
2 cups = 1 pint
2 pints = 1 litre
½ inch = 1 centimetre
1 inch = 2 centimetres

Baking Pan Sizes

American	Metric
8x1½-inch round baking pan tin	20x4-centimetre sandwich or cake
9x1½-inch round baking pan cake	23x3.5-centimetre sandwich or
11x7x1½-inch baking pan	28x18x4-centimetre baking pan
13x9x2-inch baking pan	32.5x23x5-centimetre baking pan
2-quart rectangular baking dish	30x19x5-centimetre baking pan
15x10x2-inch baking pan	38x25.5x2.5-centimetre baking pan (Swiss roll tin)
9-inch pie plate	22x4- or 23x4-centimetre pie plate
7- or 8-inch springform pan	18- or 20-centimetre springform or loose-bottom cake tin
9x5x3-inch loaf pan	23x13x6-centimetre or 2-pound narrow loaf pan or paté tin
1½-quart casserole	1.5-litre casserole
2-quart casserole	2-litre casserole

Oven Temperature Equivalents

Fahrenheit Setting	Celsius Setting*	Gas Setting
300°F	150°C	Gas Mark 2
325°F	160°C	Gas Mark 3
350°F	180°C	Gas Mark 4
375°F	190°C	Gas Mark 5
400°F	200°C	Gas Mark 6
425°F	220°C	Gas Mark 7
450°F	230°C	Gas Mark 8
Broil		Grill

*Electric and gas ovens may be calibrated using Celsius. However, increase the Celsius setting 10 to 20 degrees when cooking above 160°C with an electric oven. For convection or forced-air ovens (gas or electric), lower the temperature setting 10°C when cooking at all heat levels.